"One prick to burst a bubble"

and other articles
by

Paul Gilbert

D1638907

For Mum and Dad with love

Braiswick
Felixstowe, Suffolk

ISBN 978-0-9557008-4-2

British Library Cataloguing in Publication Data
available.

Cover by Oomph Design

Printed in England by Lightning Source

Braiswick is an imprint of Catherine Aldous Design Ltd

Index

Foreword by Colonel Bob Stewart DSO

Personal responsibility is a crucial building block of successful people everywhere and that certainly applies to lawyers operating in both public and corporate environments. Such self-imposed accountability is a constant background theme throughout Paul Gilbert's second volume of essays. He is so right to emphasise it. As the British United Nations Commander in Bosnia in 1992 – 93 the buck stopped with me in almost every sense. The shortest time it ever took for me to seek approval or guidance from my superior commander was an hour and a half. In the fast pace of the Balkan wars such a delay meant any advice or support given had normally been well overtaken by events. I had to take decisions and stand by them.

Accepting responsibility for your own actions is a matter of integrity, self-pride and professionalism. On many occasions now I have listened to Paul Gilbert explaining these points as he has coached young lawyers in the art of becoming highly rated, valuable members of legal management teams. He believes deeply that lawyers must not be backroom merchants who keep their heads down when the action gets fierce. His vision is that they should be fighters right in the thick of tricky activities who lead from the front in both thought and deed. To Paul, being a lawyer is not a safe sedentary profession. Sometimes real courage to say or do the right thing is required too. Paul personally exemplifies this approach. His professionalism, knowledge and integrity shine through in all he says or writes about acquiring the skills to succeed.

Paul Gilbert is a passionate lawyer and he recognises that passion for what it means to be a lawyer is that vital drive which fuels really effective people. Such passion is also directly connected to strength of conviction. Lawyers, Paul feels, have a responsibility to provide conviction and a firm opinion on what needs to be done. Personally I cannot think of any really good professional who does not exhibit at least a bit of passion whether they are politicians, military officers, pop stars or whatever. Surely that applies just as much to members of the legal profession as well?

Lawyers who exhibit little commitment, enthusiasm or passion are unlikely to have a sizeable fan-base amongst colleagues or clients. A dour, unenthusiastic, dispassionate and unresponsive demeanour is hardly the best way to inspire others. But we human beings are funny creatures. In my time I have met some very grim, unfriendly people who have managed to reach high places. One army general I knew had a brilliant brain and was a hugely accomplished tactician, but he was also taciturn, severe and very dull company. Yet he must have had a sense of humour. At one Staff College dinner party an officer's wife sat next to him. He said nothing, ignored her and just stared into space. Eventually the officer's wife said, 'You know I have been bet ten pounds that I can get you to say more than three words to me during dinner.' The General looked at her without any warmth, announced 'You lost' and didn't speak to her again during the meal!

Sitting back and awaiting developments before pondering action is poor practice and most definitely not Paul Gilbert's style. He suggests that the best lawyers are those who seize the initiative even if this may be a trifle risky at times. Lawyers, he believes, are people who should make things happen. After all, doing things as they have always been done is hardly conducive to changing the price of fish.

So the best lawyers are likely to be those not afraid to take decisions. Easy decisions are easy, but what defines a top-rater is his or her ability to advocate or even make the tough choices. Hopefully most such options will be the right ones, but they are likely to be wrong quite often too. In the Army I never blamed officers who made mistakes or poor decisions unless it became a trend. In my view there is one crime greater than continually making wrong decisions and that is the failure to make any at all.

Everyone knows that any briefing should be explained simply and to the point. Yet too often we can all be guilty of verbosity – and I understand this even applies to some lawyers! Winston Churchill frequently demanded planning briefings about wartime issues on one sheet of paper. Dwight D Eisenhower was another advocate of the short, precise brief. He used it both as Supreme Allied Commander and later as President of the United States. Apparently a one-page approach is also used by Sir Philip Green, owner of BHS and Arcadia Group. On such occasions it seems Green ensures all the facts he needs are on one side of paper. If problems as complex as those faced by Churchill and Eisenhower, as well as Philip Green in business today, can be simplified in that way, why shouldn't lesser mortals take note?

Paul Gilbert detests arrogance in any form, yet he knows that sometimes it is an accusation flung at lawyers. Normally it has little foundation, but occasionally it does. Intellectual snobbery or simply some feeling of being rather special compared with others is anathema to Paul, who strongly feels lawyers should be very much players in the game rather than detached observers of it. Those people who ignore the need to relate properly to colleagues or clients have simply not got it.

As a brand-new Second Lieutenant in 1970 I visited British Military Headquarters, West Berlin. Suddenly, Major General the Earl Cathcart, the General Officer Commanding and cousin of the Queen Mother, appeared in the corridor. I remember trying to shrink away, but couldn't do so before he reached me. As the 'great man' passed me, a lowly junior officer, he said 'Hello, Bob'. I had only met him once before and I was really surprised he remembered me. But what he did next had even greater impact. The General continued down the corridor and saw a German cleaning lady scrubbing the steps. He stopped, knelt down beside her and using her name, asked in German, how her sick husband was feeling. General Cathcart clearly understood his need to relate properly to everyone and their issues – no matter how grand he may have been.

Remembering not to get over-impressed by position, yours or anyone else's, and being considerate to all colleagues is another important theme that runs through Paul's excellent essays.

Since their start I have been lucky enough to attend every LBC Wise Counsel seminar held at Queens' College, Cambridge. Paul Gilbert has been lead mentor on each occasion and the feedback from lawyers at all sessions has been amazingly good – principally because of his knowledge, approach and personality. To me Paul Gilbert's words in this second Wise Counsel collection of essays encapsulate much of what was discussed and highlighted in those seminars. These essays are a window onto the very best business practice for modern public and corporate lawyers. In many ways Paul Gilbert's book is a unique insight into how lawyers should behave and I cannot commend it highly enough.

Introduction

This is the second volume of Paul Gilbert's articles, all of which have been previously published in national and international legal journals including Legal Week, The Law Society Gazette, In Brief, Without Prejudice and by Lexis Nexis and PLC. They were written between June 2007 and June 2009.

The collection provides an insight into the challenges and opportunities for lawyers at this most uncertain of times, but is often much more a heartfelt rant by a man who clearly needs to get some things off his chest. I am delighted you are indulging him!

The first volume of Paul's collected articles, called "Wise Counsel", and his first book "Head2Head – Client Relationship Management: The Client's View" are both currently available from on-line retailers and direct from LBC Wise Counsel (at www.lbcwisecounsel.com).

Geoffrey Williams
Chairman, LBC Wise Counsel

1. The Power of Brand

If you are not into marketing, then the notion of rebranding can seem like a vacuous and pointless expense. As the old (adapted) joke goes: Question – "How do you make a small fortune from rebranding?" Answer – "Start with a big one."

But if you admire the immediate recognition and values associated with names such as Nike or Microsoft or Ferrari, then maybe you believe investment in creating a great brand (and therefore rebranding) is an essential wealth creating opportunity.

The argument has always polarised opinion, with some consumers adamant that they are not influenced by advertising, while others are brand junkies, buying almost anything if it has the right label.

In a different context and on a different scale opinion is also polarised in the legal services market. Detractors argue that rebranding is about little more than vanity. They say that the silver-backed gorillas of the legal profession have made enough money now - that was relatively easy; now these big hitters want to define their legacy. They want to define the identity of their businesses, then memorialise it. Seduced by the power of brand they pursue the corporate world's elixir – a product and values that speak for themselves.

The advocates of rebranding preach that rebranding is the essential evolutionary step for legal services businesses. It will become a pre-requisite for establishing quality and awareness among clients and potential clients in an ultra competitive world. We don't chose between Burger King and MacDonalds because of our forensic analysis of their products' ingredients, but because (usually) our children are attracted to what the brand tells them about the experience of going to each place.

Establishing a good quality brand will also help price maintenance by association with values that define an ethical basis for quality, creativity and value for money. Not a pointless, vanity driven waste of money, therefore, but critical strategic insight by true leaders.

So where does this debate take us?

It is obvious to anyone who takes a look at the state of things today that legal services operate in a market in which the pace of change is quickening all the time and which is driven by the following factors:

The continuous introduction of technology that has not only made the world a quicker, more transparent place to live and work in, but which has also shortened timelines in transactions, in litigation etc. and commoditised quite complex corporate and commercial matters.

- The rise and rise of procurement style purchasing of legal services with its emphasis on cost reduction, defined and measurable service performance indicators and routine, systematic review.

- Niche players finding that excellence is not dependent on size, thus creating a market for legal services away from the globalised monoliths.

- Mid-sized firms realising that merger or significant internal structural change are their main routes to surviving the next five years.

- An in-house legal community that is more self-confident, of a significantly higher quality and much more demanding than it has ever been. In-house lawyer act as gate-keepers to their businesses, filtering inefficient outsourcing and holding the legal spend budgets for their companies.

There are other factors as well, but in these five points it is clear that change is rapid and real and that perhaps above everything else there are fewer and fewer of the old certainties in legal services.

When the world is in such a state of flux, what is needed is great leadership, a confident proposition and a genuine understanding of how to adapt and exploit old and new markets - hence the push for a brand identity that supports these values and helps to establish the credentials of one player against another.

In the days when the choice was between Bloggs, Higgins and Bloggs at one end of the town and Herbert, Humphrey and Harris at the other, brand did not matter at all. Now, however, we could expect "BHB legal" or "3H" (as they would surely now be known) to have marketing teams, business development teams, brochures, websites, seminar programmes, on-line tools, PR professionals, focus groups etc. - all geared to help develop, define and live up to the brand that each firm believes will help secure its future.

We can all scoff a little at the fortunes spent on fine (even imperceptible) nuances of shade and typeface that caricature some efforts, but what everyone is seeking is that edge that makes their firm more memorable.

In my judgment we are still at the start of the change cycle. It is very difficult to predict what will happen and when, but even a casual observer would think that there was much more to follow.

The advent of external investment, which, in the UK at least, is close to becoming a reality, and the increasing pressure on both buyers and suppliers to articulate value are just two of the pressure points.

While the end game is some way off, we know now what has to be done to survive and thrive in the new environment:

- Firms cannot simply proclaim excellence in legal expertise as a point of differentiation.

- The values a firm holds dear may be a factor that resonates, but it will be the consistency with which a firm lives up to those values that tests their credibility the most.

- Articulating value and innovation in both pricing and risk sharing will be key factors as well - not just a great service, but an incentivised and targeted service that business people will see has made a genuine contribution to the bottom line.

- Value-added services that are not "given-away", but which are part of the service proposition, leveraged and thought through, meeting the real needs of the client.

- Soft skills (relationship management, presentation, communication etc.) that are so well trained and so finely honed that nothing is left to chance.

So is rebranding about vanity? Well, for a few misguided souls it might be. It is, however, far more important than that.

For most firms their brand will become a key part of their client proposition. For most firms investment in the brand, identifying the values that define the essence of service and integrity, will become an essential exercise in the months and years to come.

2. The Perception Conundrum

I n the UK just now we are in the middle of the holiday season.
When I was a child I very fondly remember my summers as warm, sunny, full of friends and games and just about the best of times a boy could have. Now as a parent, summer holidays are a logistical feat (nightmare?) as child-care, holiday planning and work commitments conspire to make the whole period seem more often like an ordeal than a pleasure.

Isn't it funny how we can all view the same world differently if we have a different perspective on it? I am always fascinated by how these everyday situations throw up contrary perceptions and how we work all the time to manage perception without even thinking about it...I also find that it is very often in these ordinary events that we can find the best clues to solving the extraordinary.

About a year ago I was hired by a well known law firm to undertake some research on what different groups within the firm felt about how the firm was doing. The firm wanted to develop a more consistent approach to internal communication and to external presentation of its values and proposition - in fact generally to improve the way it behaved as a business. My work was to help them identify the base line they had already established (on the principle that before you can navigate any journey you have to have a pretty good idea where you are starting from).

As an example of what we found, here are two statements from two people within the firm, one a partner, one a trainee.

"Communication internally isn't good enough; we hardly get to know anything before it happens. Decisions are made in a vacuum. I just keep my head down and get on with my job."

"Communication is good. We work really hard to keep all our people informed. We don't always agree with what happens, but at least you know why."

It isn't a surprise to find partners and junior team members having a different view on communication; however, the very interesting fact about these two statements is that the first was made by the partner and the second by the trainee.

Interesting perhaps, but, frankly, so what? Well, good question; the "so what?" was to see if such a perception conundrum was repeated elsewhere and what might lie behind it.

Before I explain this, let me explain something else which lies behind a lot of my work. In all the time I have been working both as a lawyer and latterly as a consultant, I have held to two particular principles:

- First, that the vast majority of people go to their place of work to do a good job, and

- Second, that there is no reason why one set of lawyers should be any worse than another set of lawyers at communication, leadership, management and presentation (etc.).

Thus any firm or department or team has the potential to be outstanding and to be up there with the very best. The key to unlocking this potential is to find the small things that are not working well and to fix them.

Like a golf swing, a hopeless slice will give a horrible result, but it will only need the very smallest of fine adjustments to turn such miserable consequences into much more rewarding and good looking results.

Back to my assignment…

What became apparent, signalled by the quotes I have highlighted, was a perception conundrum. On the one hand a significant group of partners feeling disconnected from their business and yet a very large body of junior staff who felt the firm was a great place to work.

I could find two reasons for their different perspectives.

The first was that the partners had for the last three years invested significantly in the firm's infrastructure, recruiting excellent quality trainees, refurbishing their offices, investing in technology. This had obviously required some financial sacrifice on their part. The second reason was that the firm had been quite successful in this period as well and was attracting new and more important work.

Trainees saw investment in the firm, career development and a success story unfolding; partners saw more work, less money in their pockets and a disrupted office with builders and contractors everywhere.

I saw a firm on the brink of a very important breakthrough, a firm that could take very important strides forward, a firm that could be the next big success story.

The challenge for the firm's leadership team was to ensure that all the hard work did not start to unravel just at the point when the reward might be in sight. Key to confirming the progress made was now to ensure that internally their success to date was understood, that the plan was restated and those who might be losing patience were re-energised. They were on the right path.

Change, as we all know, is never easy; leadership is never easy and well intentioned slogans to work harder and smarter are not the answer when a team is weary with effort; but insightful, empathetic and certain steps along a well communicated plan will increase the opportunity for success.

It is not the hard work which undoes good intentions; it is not having confidence that all the hard work will be worth it. This is a communication issue and it is one that persists throughout a project or a relationship – it is one we neglect at our peril.

Finally, I have to say that in the case in point I also saw something of the conundrum I mentioned in the opening lines of this article. The child's perception of summer can be very different from the parents' perception of the very same summer, however good the communication!

3. Out of my depth?

I was having coffee the other day with an in-house lawyer newly appointed to her first role; she was interesting and thoughtful and her conversation was engaging and full of optimism, but then she said something that made me pause for thought. She said, "I am really uncomfortable doing new things; I always feel that I am so much out of my depth."

As a familiar metaphor "out of my depth" is an easy to use and every day turn of phrase, but pause for a moment to reflect on these words; taken literally they carry a significant burden and are laden with discomfort.

The phrase, for me, conjures up an image of flailing limbs in a hostile sea, lungs bursting with pain and a helpless surrender to a certain end. These words "out of my depth" seem to indicate the sort of deep-seated and personal discomfort that would travel to the pit of one's stomach in an instant.

Such innocuous words perhaps, but such horrible connotations; no wonder the newly appointed in-house lawyer was reluctant to try new things if it made her feel out of her depth.

The fear of change which she was indicating, both at an organisational level and for very many of us as individuals, is a widespread and very real phenomenon. To be good at change we need more than to be able to articulate why change is potentially a good thing: we also need to plan to overcome this almost phobic reflex response to the thought of change.

In short, we need a different way of thinking, a different metaphor.

How would we feel, for example, if we were not really out of our depth at all? What if we were absolutely at the same depth we normally operate in? Would it not appear a more comfortable experience if we could be convinced of this as a new reality?

I am convinced that for most changes we make (or are forced to make), it is not the depth that has changed, but the fact that we are swimming in unfamiliar waters where the landmarks on the shoreline are different.

And if that is the case, we are not going to drown; we will be perfectly fine in fact and we will have all the skills and the experience we need to survive in our new surroundings and maybe even to thrive.

Consider this thought (and a different metaphor again) - when you drive your car to a new place, to somewhere you have never been before, you can still physically drive the car – you have not forgotten how to steer or how to change gear; but you may have to concentrate a little more and you may have to prepare the way a little more thoroughly as well.

The discomfort we feel by labelling how we feel as "out of our depth" effectively elevates change from being, in my driving analogy, a need for a little more concentration as we look for somewhere to park, to a near death experience in the freezing waters of the North Atlantic (and that is also now a mixed metaphor!).

So how should we combat this fear of change?

I would like to suggest a ten point comfort blanket - ten points not to falsely reassure, but to put into context what most change is really about; ten points to help us manage our own emotional response to change.

While all change can be described in terms of negative outcomes like more work, more disruption, unknown consequences etc., it is also true that most change can be described with positive consequences as well. Change teaches us to adapt, to see opportunity, to develop skills etc.. Change itself is a potentially a very positive experience - as Albert Einstein said:

"There is nothing that is a more certain sign of insanity than to do the same thing over and over again and expect the results to be different..."

9

1. Change is also inevitable in any event – it is a constant in our lives and we cope every single day with any amount of it. Work priorities move, supermarkets run out of something we want, the garage is closed on the way home, the TV schedulers move the kick-off time of the football...etc. Change is not a problem for any of us, but what we are less good at is unfamiliar change.

2. Unfamiliar change takes us by surprise and often causes three responses - to flee, freeze or fight. All three responses, however, are emotional and obstructive and none of them help us deal with either the change process or the consequences of change. If they become a pattern of behaviour, we will always struggle. Knowing this is the start of dealing with it differently.

3. Change is rarely destructive of itself. The fact that we may feel somewhat uncomfortable is often the necessary prerequisite for personal development and progress; while being comfortable can be, conversely, indicative of a slow decline into complacency and decay.

4. That is not to say, however, that change in every instance is necessarily a good thing. Change for its own sake might well be disruptive and change must always be well planned, well communicated and well managed. Therefore, we should not accept change in an unthinking way and we must preserve a reasoned opportunity to push back.

5. Sometimes, for example, we also make the mistake of evaluating the benefits of change, but ignoring the benefits of the status quo. When evaluating the impact of change, we must also evaluate the impact of the status quo. By developing our understanding of the reality of our current circumstances we can better inform the debate (for or against) change, but without the emotional, destructive response. Relevant questions are:

a) Is the status quo rewarding, challenging and fun?

b) Is the status quo a permanent stable state or is it, too, merely temporary?

c) Do our colleagues and friends look at change in the same way as we do? If there is no consensus about the viability of the status quo, what are they likely to want to change and when?

d) Can we exert some influence over the status quo? If we can, is that influence any more than the influence we can exert over change? If we have influence, change is more likely to have positive outcomes.

e) Is it better to change positively and with energy or to sit tight in the equivalent of a brace crash position and hope the moment will pass?

6. Change is rarely, if ever, made to annoy or upset us; there is, therefore, precious little to be gained by arguing emotionally against change. Even if our concerns are well intentioned, an argument based on emotions will appear Luddite (or worse) and definitely not a good place to begin negotiations. So we should argue facts, argue logic and argue better alternatives. Not all change is good, but bad change occurs because we lose our perspective and create distracting and pointless arguments which are bound to fail.

7. When change is contemplated, opportunity is created too. It's like a chemical reaction. If we seek out the opportunity and judge the benefit of the opportunity before we resist the change, many possibilities are revealed.

8. Life (as the old cliché goes) is a journey, but it should not always be a Sunday afternoon ride down a familiar lane to the same old places. While some days like this are good, no one should want their whole life

to be like it. Let the journey be a mixture of the old and the new, the fast and the slow, the risk- free and, occasionally, the risky too.

9. Never again should we have the automatic response that we will be "out of our depth" with change simply because it is unfamiliar. Most likely you are swimming just fine. The shoreline a little different perhaps, but the swimmer in control, comfortable and maybe even enjoying the new views.

Of course articles like this are bound to simplify things too much and it is always easier to say these things than to actually do them. However, while change is not easy and is only ever relished by a very few, it should not be so daunting. What we must always try to do is to reflect on how we will make change work for us.

The in-house lawyer with whom I shared a coffee, like all of us, has the capacity to change and to take advantage of the opportunity that change brings. Enjoy the swim.

4. My lawyer is great... really great

It would have been lovely, but I am not sure the line "My lawyer is great, really great" was ever used about me. I am absolutely certain it was never used about my legal abilities and I suspect that is probably true of most lawyers.

Can you, for example, imagine a client of yours giving you a call today -

"Hey Bill, thanks for the email - just been reading the suggested amendments to the I.T. contract. Great work, you old devil you...

"What a super little warranty clause you snuck in there... a real cheeky little number; I just love the way that 'must' plays with the dominant 'best endeavours' - absolutely fabulous. You know, of all the lawyers we could use, your standard precedent clauses are just the BEST!"

Let's face it, it will probably never happen.

But what does happen, and often (I hope), is that clients will say,

"Thank you for getting the report to me in time and making the points understandable."

Or "Thank you for keeping to the agreed budget."

Or "Thank you for just being there when I need someone on my side."

And all these sentiments go to the very essence of what being a great lawyer is about. It isn't about the law you know, it's about the relationships you develop and the value people attribute to the quality of the relationship.

Take this as a proposition – the time you knew the most law was the week before your law finals examinations! Were you a great lawyer then?

And from that point onwards we all slowly let go of most of the legal knowledge we ever had. By the time we reach Partner or General Counsel, there would not be a hope in hell of us sitting and passing a law exam; yet at that point we are at our most self-confident and probably at our best.

The critical point, and the point which underpins all our success, is that for the great majority of the time, for most of our clients and for most of the work we do, it is not our knowledge of the law that the client is valuing. Instead they are valuing accessibility, presentation, empathy, efficiency, timeliness, relevancy, passion, interest and, above all, trust.

This is the essence of being a great lawyer. What is more, these are not characteristics that are the exclusive preserve of an elite few, with brains the size of planets, who practise in the legal stratosphere. In my judgement these are the characteristics that we can all live up to, every single day, with every single matter and for every single client.

A great deal of the work I do is helping lawyers fulfil their potential to become great lawyers and that means developing the rounded skills set that is essential to do this.

And it is not easy. We typically find, for example, that 80% of training budgets are spent on legal update training and only 20% is spent on other essential skills. What a waste of money.

It still surprises me how often people go on courses that simply fulfil the compulsory requirement to gather the quota of professional development hours they need, with no real thought to the usefulness of the programme.

It still surprises me how often people complain about the inconvenience of training and the cost of training, without ever thinking about the absolute requirement to invest effectively in their personal development.

It still surprises me how many delegates don't turn up to events or leave them at the first opportunity because they want to miss the traffic or meet a friend or go shopping.

Maybe all of this is a reflection on the paucity of training content and quality – but maybe it is because lawyers do not invest enough care and attention in thinking about what their training needs really are and how those needs should be met.

Just maybe there is also a subconscious realisation that legal update training by itself is much less necessary for most people and it therefore gets the treatment it deserves.

Perhaps lawyers should look more for skills training and, for a change, find the events that will give them the wherewithal that will cause their clients to begin to think they also had a great lawyer working for them.

Okay, I know I am ranting…rant over!

But it is truly important to make sure that each one of us takes full responsibility for our personal development and training. It seems to me to be absolutely crucial that we do not just rely on our Training Department or the Human Resources professionals to do this for us (however well intentioned they are). In the end it is our career, not theirs.

And it is not just about formal training; having a great network to support us is just as important. We all need to have people we are close to whose opinions we value and trust. Some people shy away from the term "mentoring", but whatever we call it, we need to sense-check our feelings and our approach sometimes and mentoring, in my opinion, is something we should strive to institutionalise in all our businesses.

So this is what we must all do – we must develop our internal and external networks; we must learn to seek out and to act on constructive feedback; we must seek opportunities to present and to write in order to hone our communication skills; we must develop our capacity to work efficiently, to manage meetings expertly, to keep our commitments and to articulate value; we must do all we can to align our expertise to the needs and interests of our clients.

This is not a wish-list, not some aspirational counsel of perfection; this is eminently attainable and within reach for every single one of us and it is also genuinely the stuff of being a great lawyer.

5. Mind the gap...

Talking to one City law firm partner the other day, I was left a little nonplussed by an assertion of economic hardship... "You would not believe," he said, "how hard it is for us to attract and retain the best young talent. It is just getting to be so expensive."

I felt that I should point out that many of his clients might also be aware of the issue given that their hourly rates were now typically 20% higher than eighteen months ago. We also both noted that the age of the £1000 per hour partner was here despite all this "fearsome competition"'.

Is it only me who wonders how increased competition has meant that the cost for the consumer is going up? Doesn't this suggest that something isn't quite right from the client side in this model?

I also wonder whether this impacts at all on how in-house lawyers see the world.

I wonder, for example, whether a seven years qualified in-house lawyer feels any pang of regret when the two years qualified associate is paid so much more.

I wonder, when the General Counsel is beaten up (again) by the Finance Director for yet another adverse variance on the legal spend management accounts, whether the law firm feels that irritation too.

I also wonder, when those same law firms announce they are moving to even swankier premises (where their new glass-fronted edifices have so much empty space in the reception area they could double up as hangers for a small country's air force), whether their clients ever think if it might just be getting a bit, you know, too expensive.

It concerns me and I think the legal services profession has got to be careful, because I am not sure much of this is sustainable for very much longer.

It is undoubtedly true that the professionalism, care and quality of much of the client proposition has improved in recent years. Debates about value-add no longer result in blank expressions, but are seen by all as a key strategic lever to enhance the client's perception of value across the whole relationship. I also think that for many individual lawyers, the service they give is quite brilliant being both expert and empathetic.

This is all excellent, but on the downside, costs continue to rise, sometimes sharply, and are too often disconnected from plausible conversations about productivity improvements, enhanced services or greater added value. Worse than this is the persistent damage done by clinging to a basis of charging that goes back decades – the hourly rate.

I have heard every justification for it; people say the system is well known (but that is like knowing somewhere is an accident black spot; it doesn't make it safe to drive there); they say it is too difficult to put a price on variable factors (so fifty years of data on thousands of files means we still don't know the length of a piece of string – not really credible is it?) or they say it is too difficult to change IT systems (roll on private equity investment in that case).

A great many in-house lawyers also defend the system. I am often told that it is the only consistent method of charging that allows a comparison across firms. But it allows them to compare £375 with £400; it doesn't compare efficiency, value, risk or quality.

Meanwhile law firms get all het up as they take on the increased costs of trying to secure the best talent, but then relieve their anxiety with a compensating entry on the other side of the profit and loss account! Super strategy; if only all their clients could do the same.

The point is that, while many will find reasons not to change, it doesn't mean the system is fair, competitive or in the long term interests of the client or the law firm. In the end, loyalty to a relationship will matter less and less; it will be reserved for those few matters where cost really does not matter or where it is a significant stress purchase.

For everything else, the inexorable creep of commoditisation and the rise (and rise) of procurement style disciplines will simply demand that pricing becomes much more transparent.

If law firms want to compete in five years time, the objective today should be to invest in the systems that can quantify and qualify how much the services they offer will cost. The firms that can genuinely offer transparent pricing will be the firms that are most likely to compete for work.

They will also be the firms most able to diversify their proposition by unbundling their service and joining with the client in a much more creative partnership.

We are already seeing how some clients want to appoint a single law firm to manage significant volumes of work across many subject disciplines. This, by accident or design, creates the potential for the much sought after seamless service as the line blurs between what is an internal and an external legal service.

Transparent pricing, seamless service, great management information, significant investment in value-add, confident risk-sharing and long-term investment in a mutual gains relationship - I was writing about this five years ago and now it is happening. And I firmly believe it will become the model of choice for a great many clients because it will be very attractive to business (if not to the lawyers).

As one chief executive said to me recently, "This company has one strategic adviser, my Finance Director has one external auditor, my Marketing Director has one advertising agency, why does my General Counsel need a dozen law firms when one would surely do?"

There is a lesson here for the whole profession.

6. Draughty halls and cold showers...The alternative way to customer satisfaction

I was standing patiently in line last week waiting for the man in front of me to finish his diatribe. I was waiting to check-out of the hotel I had been staying in... he was not happy to go quietly.

It was a really nice hotel; newly refurbished, all mod-cons, digital this and digital that, 24 hour everything and hot and cold running customer service experiences driven through every "Have a nice day" interaction.

The man in front of me, however, was in no mood to recognise any of this. Apparently at 4:05am he had been woken by the sound of other guests returning rather noisily to their room after a presumably cheerful night out.

He then had the inconvenience of finding that the incompetents behind the scenes had delivered a copy of The Times to his room and not the Daily Mail he had ordered the night before.

The final straw for him was that this morning the "executive lounge" was full to overflowing when he tried to get his complimentary breakfast (despite his elite card carrying status) and instead he was re-directed to the main restaurant...

For all this hardship he now anticipated a grand gesture. I think I heard him say (although obviously I was doing my best not to hear any of it), "If you expect me to come here again, I don't expect you to charge me for this bloody awful night."

It is hard to imagine why apparently minor irritations should create such vitriol, but it serves as a counterpoint to something I have noticed about a residential programme we run for in-house lawyers at Queens' College, Cambridge.

Queens' College provides perhaps one of the most stunningly beautiful settings for study anywhere in the world. It is jaw-droppingly lovely.

When I first saw the rooms we were able to use for our event, I knew we would be creating a unique learning experience that would live long in the memory. But I also knew we might have a bit of a challenge with the accommodation for our delegates.

The rooms for the delegates are student accommodation. They are very clean and charming in their way. But they are utilitarian, functional and basic. Showers might be described as intermittent. There are no TVs in the rooms, no mini bars, no shag-pile carpet.

So at every event we brace ourselves for critical comments about the accommodation, but the strange thing is that at every event we get nothing negative at all.

Instead delegates and speakers tell us it adds to the uniqueness of the event; that it is really good "fun" to remember what being a student was like; that it is nice we are "all mixed in together" and "Who needs a TV when the company is this good?"

The Old Hall at Queens' College is the centre for our event. It is an inspiring venue, but one which frankly has lousy acoustics and a wicked draught. The delegates and speakers love it, however, and enjoy every second of being there.

In significant contrast the big city law firms now go to great lengths to make every aspect of the client environment as perfect as it possibly can be.

One city firm (I hear) has just employed a second biscuit chef!

Surely to goodness I hope someone somewhere did not present a PowerPoint slideshow on the competitive advantage of biscuits. Even so, one knows that somewhere there is a budget and a committee behind it. God save us!

I wonder now whether sometimes we have so mismanaged expectation that we are preoccupied with the wrapping and not the substance. Could it be that we might want to dazzle with the perfection of our environment, but have lost sight of the humanity and soul that is at the heart of every meaningful experience?

After all, we all know that the law is a relationship business, where trust and credibility have to be at the forefront of the desired outcomes.

I am not going to hire or fire a firm for the quality of their biscuits and I am sure no one ever will. I will even put up with a cold and draughty meeting room, but what is crucial is to feel important, to be part of something where people care, where time is taken to find out what I want and need and to help me get there as effectively as possible.

Lawyers must never trade on the vanity of their architecture, but on the sincerity of their vocation.

Show me a law firm that truly cares for its clients and those clients will never seriously criticise the decor, the absence of free-trade coffee or the quality of the freebie pads and pens.

In the end we all want the same things and in the long list of what we want, nice biscuits might not be the deal-breaker.

My ranting man in the line at the hotel would probably have coped with The Times instead of the Daily Mail, and might not have minded his relocated breakfast, provided he felt people really did care and really were trying to make his stay important. Instead I think he just felt that his experience, despite the trappings of comfort and joy, was that of occupying a soulless twilight zone where the most important fact the hotel staff knew about him was his credit card number.

7. Changing the way we change

No New Year is complete without a thought to introducing some change into our lives... it might be personal (I will try to lose the weight I lost once, before the weight I have just put on) or professional (I will prepare properly for all team meetings and not treat them as an inconvenience to my hectic schedule of assorted crisis management events) or even one that combines the two (I will try to make some time to consider how my own career should develop and not expect the next promotion to be the responsibility of someone else).

In all these endeavours, however, we seem to continually risk failure; not because we have a lack of ambition, not because we lack the skills to implement our ideas and not because we are lazy. No, we risk failure for two very significant reasons:

- Reason 1: We are, as we always have been, habitually poor at communicating with each other about what we want and expect of others.

- Reason 2: We do not develop competitive consequences for the changes we want to make and instead rely, excessively so, on announcing what we want (as if change could happen by proclamation!).

It is at once both startling and predictable that, in this age of hundreds of television channels and interactive mass media and with the first SMS text and email generation in the workforce, we still mismanage communication.

The fact that we can all communicate so easily with each other and in so many more ways does not mean we engage, persuade or encourage. Often all we do is succeed in creating a wall of noise, but to be heard is not the same thing as to be listened to.

This is familiar territory for us all, but it is territory we must constantly revisit if we are to achieve what we hope to achieve; but before expanding on this theme, let me introduce my second less familiar theme – that of "competitive consequences". A writer I admire hugely is the American behaviour expert Aubrey Daniels, whose work includes "Bringing Out The Best In People"; it is he who best describes this idea. An analogy will help to explain:

You are sat at your computer working on a long and complicated document. You have been there for some time when you hear that familiar ping of a new email message arrive:

a) Ignore the new message and refocus all your concentration on the complicated document you have been working on?

b) Flick immediately to your in-basket to see who the sender of the new email message is?

c) Continue to work on the complicated document, but hear voices in your head telling you to go to your in-basket instead?!

I will not presume to speak for you, but I can tell you that I would hardly ever be an a) person. I am mostly b) and occasionally c). As a result I am distracted and probably less productive.

One of the keys to understanding this behaviour is to realise that there are no competitive consequences for my choice of b) or c); and so I am easily pulled into a way of behaving inefficiently despite the fact that I can rationally consider the outcome to be inefficient and distracting.

Imagine then, rather fancifully perhaps, putting in place competitive consequences so that, if I switch from my long complicated document to my new email, I will receive a mild but noticeably uncomfortable electric shock! In these circumstances I might think twice about flitting back and forth. Equally, if I were to receive a small but desired bonus for finishing my complicated document in a certain time (and accurately, then that too might discourage my distraction.

And the reason the inefficient behaviour is now more likely to be influenced is that there are competitive consequences. Let us take a more typical change initiative.

I often see the result of well-intentioned change programmes where the level of satisfaction for those involved remains stubbornly low. Typically we see that there is a reorganisation of roles, a bit of downsizing and some change to professional duties. All those who are affected by the changes are intelligent and thoughtful people who will not dismiss change out of hand; everyone generally wants to co-operate. Those in charge of the initiative often go to some lengths to set up the change programme with a report published, plans developed and consulted on and sometimes even an oversight committee formed…

And yet in seven out of ten similar situations "poor communication" is held up as a reason why change was not implemented successfully. Closer analysis will often show that the messages were reasonably clear and well crafted, but that they were too complicated, too long and too far apart; and, crucially, that they failed to resonate at those levels where people had to be persuaded to act differently.

Even closer examination will show that so much time and energy had been spent on the message that hardly any thought had been given to setting up competitive consequences. This is not just a question of putting in place a blunt two-dimensional incentive (although such incentives clearly can work); rather we need to have a proper insight into what is actually happening around us so that we can put in place something much more thoughtful and clever to influence change.

After all, the behaviour we each exhibit every single day is behaviour we practise every single day; not surprisingly we get very good at it. Clearly to change such behaviour needs much more than a few communications (however well crafted) and much more effort than any project group on its own will ever be able to deliver.

What is needed is a level of practical engagement that not only makes communication relevant and resonant, but which also creates for those involved meaningful, competitive consequences that are thoughtful, measured and effective in order to reward and encourage change.

It is this combination of resonant communication and competitive consequences that helps to secure change. Anything else risks the same ending as a great many other failed change programmes. So, if this New Year you are tempted to embark on personal or professional change, this time, take a little more time to focus not just on the message and how it will be received, but also on the sort of consequences that need to be built into the change process to give the best possible encouragement for change to actually happen.

8. In less than 100 words

Ireceived an innocuous little message the other day-
"Can you please tell us in less than 100 words what
you do?" It was for a law firm's newsletter and I was
getting some advance billing for a series of workshops
that would be running in a few weeks time. "Easy" I
thought, but I soon discovered that it was anything but
easy; and now I put the same challenge to you.

It reminded me of one of the exercises in my presentation
skills programme that asks delegates to imagine they have
stepped into a lift to find that the only other person in it is
their Chief Executive, who then asks, "So, tell me, what do
you do?" The delegate has about twenty seconds to make
a positive impression.

Very often lawyers describe what they do by the
specialism they have; for example, you might hear some
say "I work in Employment" or "I'm a litigator" etc...

Similarly in the presentations law firms make to join
new client panels I will often read that law firms employ
"XX commercial lawyers" in "XX countries"; and while
it is interesting to know this, it is hardly ever a point of
differentiation between competitor firms, who can say
almost exactly the same things in such strikingly similar
ways!

So could you describe what you do in 100 words or
fewer and make it sound valuable and interesting?

Such a communication might, of course, change
according to the audience (your mum or your boss), but
in essence, in the context of your professional value and
expertise, what do you do that would make someone
(client or colleague) want to invest more of their precious
time and energy engaging with you?

As you ponder, you may begin to see yourself not just
as a lawyer with a subject expertise, but as any number of
things - a facilitator, a problem solver, a creative solution

finder, a shoveller of waste product! You might consider yourself a communicator, a diplomat, a trusted adviser... and so on.

And as you develop a little literary flourish in these attractive descriptions, consider as well, whether your clients and colleagues would agree with you. Not to be harsh in any way, but do they honestly and consistently see, feel and appreciate the role you now profess to have?

You see, you are far more than just a lawyer; you are all of the above (and more) and each element is visible for better or for worse, every single day. The responsibility this places on you is both to live up to the aspiration of your role and to find ways to demonstrate that you are succeeding.

Let us take just one idea and develop it: you are a creative problem solver - this is good. You should be and your colleagues and clients should want you to be; but how many problems did you solve today? This week? This month? More or fewer than you think?

What value can you ascribe to the problems you have solved? Would your colleagues and clients agree with you? Was the value you ascribe worth the effort of your time?

In what ways were your solutions creative? Would that creativity be valued by your colleagues and clients? Would they have valued a different approach? Or were they delighted with your answer and the way you reached it?

This is really important stuff, because if you cannot describe these things, please do not expect your clients and colleagues to do so for you. And if you cannot easily describe these things, you are either not doing them (at all or enough) or you need to check that you are.

It is a truism that we are valued less for our legal skills and much more for our people skills, but because it is a truism we tend to skate over its significance.

It does no harm, therefore, to remind ourselves occasionally that being "a litigator" or "an employment lawyer" is pretty much a pointless and meaningless description of what we do, when everything about our value is predicated on influencing, relationship building, communicating, facilitating, being creative and so on.

This is a good lesson.

And if you do the same in-depth analysis of all the other epithets that you would like ascribed to you, you will have a far deeper understanding of what you do, how you do it and how well you are valued for it.

I hope you can say wonderful things about yourself and your work, but we are mere mortals and we will be wracked with some self-doubt at least some of the time; my guess is that this exercise will make us pause for thought.

This is, I think, good news; it will show us gently where we might need to focus some effort, not always to be better at what we do, but to become so much better at how we do it.

So, back to the description of what you do in less than 100 words.

It still won't be easy, but it will feel good to know that you have explored the edges of what you say are good things to be, to have a better understanding of how these things are valued and to know you have areas to work on to become even better at what you do.

So the next time you step into a lift and find yourself alone with the chief executive, after you have floored him or her with your erudition, you might even ask the same question - "So, tell me, what do you do"!!!

9. Networking – Give more, seek less

We ran a networking event recently in a regional centre far, far away from the capital city. We thought lawyers would be pleased to have an opportunity to meet friends and contacts and not have to travel into London to do so. Four lawyers showed up - not so much networking, more like a blind date without the romantic subtext!

This is really interesting because we know that all lawyers value the opportunity to share ideas, to take soundings, to sense check their thinking. We also know that networking is one of the best ways to informally benchmark one's breadth of role, responsibilities, risk management and best practices - even one's salary!

And if you are a law firm associate, how else are you going to build a practice if you are not out there networking like fury.

Anyway, after the event we spoke to a few people who said they were coming but who had failed to make it on the night. The feedback was illuminating. Two people said they had been called into meetings; one said that he didn't think he would get much from it and there was a decent football match on the TV; three people thought the idea of networking, on reflection, was a bit old hat; another three said that they had forgotten it was on!

Hey ho.

Although, to an extent, I can see where they are coming from - it's a long day, you've worked hard, handled the stress, delivered a half decent service, the drive home beckons; why would you want to go and stand in a hotel meeting space, suck on a piece of bread-crumbed chicken and drink a glass of cheap wine? (Not that our events are like this obviously!)

Why would you, especially when you think you might not get much from it? After all, the people who do want to suck on warm chicken and drink cheap wine, probably aren't the people you would want to meet anyway… Right?

But this of course is to misunderstand the point of a networking event, even one as undersold as the one in question. If we approach networking as an exercise in what we will get from it, it is almost certainly doomed to fail. The skill of networking is not what one takes, it's what one gives.

Dale Carnegie said: "You can make more friends in two months by becoming interested in other people than you can in two years trying to get other people to be interested in you…"

I suspect this may all sound far too evangelical for most; so let me break this down more prosaically, because networking is an essential piece of activity and we all need to be good at it. These are my observations and I'll be very happy to talk about them with you next time we meet at a networking event!

1. Don't feel you have to go to every opening of an envelope, but if you have said you will go, make sure that you do. We all know that stuff happens and sometimes the unforeseen gets in the way; this is always understood and should never be an issue. However, getting a reputation for accepting invitations and serially failing to turn up is disrespectful to one's host and likely to reflect poorly.

2. If the whole thing feels a bit daunting, go with a colleague or friend so that when you are at the event you work as a team. Arriving alone at an unfamiliar venue and walking into a room full of unfamiliar faces is a challenging prospect to say the least; but go as a pair and it can be great fun. There is always a "safe haven" to return to and, if you work the room together, it is quite possible to move from one contact to another in a very elegant way.

3. Ask questions and **listen** to the answers; easy really, but we don't do this very well. Questions should be

open, eye contact should be made and try hard to listen to the answer. A supplementary question that builds on the initial answer shows you are engaged and interested and encourages conversation.

4. Ask the best question in the world ever! This is a big claim, but it has never failed for me. Most people, consciously or subconsciously, like to talk about what they do in the context of positive affirmation. The question should be phrased something like this: "That sounds really interesting – tell me, how did you do that?"; then relax…the next few minutes should go swimmingly!

5. Don't try to seek help or support. Whatever you do don't turn up to an event expecting to ask for help. If it happens naturally in the context of your conversation, that is fine, but it jars with most people. I once met someone who started taking notes while I was talking and asked me to repeat the names of people he thought might be able to help him. In a way he was just making sure he got accurate detail, but I felt as though I had been pick-pocketed.

6. Follow up with a thank you to the host and other "pleased to have met you" messages to those you spoke to. Courtesy counts for a lot; it will cement the recollection of your conversation with those you met and it is also a good way to pass on your contact detail without being explicit about it.

7. If/when the next invitation comes round, contact the people you met before to renew their acquaintance, even if you or they cannot make the next event. These gentle contact situations create a tone of voice around the way you work; be undemanding, interested and thoughtful. It costs virtually nothing, but helps to create a climate in which you and your contacts fit comfortably. One day you will need them and that day will be the time to benefit from your careful networking.

So the next time you are invited to a networking event, please accept and go, and whether four people or four hundred turn up with you, practise these ideas and let me know how you got on. I'd like to know.

10. Whatever you do, please don't exceed my expectations!

Have you ever filled in a customer satisfaction survey – one of those where you tick the box that best describes the service or value received? They come with a promise that it "helps us to improve our performance", although I suspect it only really helps to give the illusion that the cold-hearted, anonymous corporate edifice actually gives a damn!

The same approach is very often taken in performance and appraisal meetings as well (I am so glad I don't have to do these any more!).

"How would you rate X's communication skills? Does X: Fail to meet your expectations? Partially meet your expectations? Meet your expectations? Exceed your expectations?"

As we all know, there are seemingly endless HR generated processes and forms to complete, all designed to provide insight and enlightenment, and then there is also the obligatory debate over ranking.

How do you think lawyers relate to this sort of assessment? Yep, you would be right!

Not that lawyers are much different from the general populace I suppose, but I have to tell you that most lawyers at appraisal time are about as touchy on this subject as it is possible to get.

"What do you mean I *met* expectations?" (said with the same sort of sneering emphasis one should properly save for interviewing politicians on television).

Lawyers are trained to believe that merely by opening a file they have already added to the sum of significant human endeavour. The idea, therefore, that completing a piece of work might only *meet* expectations would be like suggesting a romantic date with Kiera Knightly might be "OK".

And where has all this HR inspired nonsense taken us? Precisely nowhere. There is no insight, no enlightenment, no wisdom, no learning; instead there is a stressful tussle over what constitutes either "meeting" or "exceeding" expectations.

It all comes flooding back - conversations going round in circles: "But I stayed late", "It ruined my weekend", "It was the other side", "The client didn't have a clue anyway", "No one works harder than me", "What more could I do?" ...and so on.

And the rather depressing point about this sterile debate is that it is the wrong debate to have anyway!

I don't want lawyers who *EXCEED* my expectations!

What the hell is the point of that? I have an expectation, you meet it, I pay you, we move on!

Exceeding expectations smacks of gilding the lily, of over-engineering, of, frankly, wasting my time and money by doing more than was necessary.

I don't want lawyers *going the extra mile*.

I want lawyers who get me safely to my destination, on time and on budget. Imagine the debate you would have with a taxi driver who cheerfully tells you, "Well sir, I am sure you will be delighted to recognise that I have gone the extra mile for you."

You see, we have been sidetracked by a sterile debate to supposedly recognise and reward excellence. Instead of that outcome, however, we have elevated and rewarded behaviour that is slightly contrived, emotive and faux-heroic to an unprecedented level and, worse, largely ignored the lawyers who, day in, day out, deliver a service that is efficient, adequate, wanted and reasonably priced.

Meeting expectations is the benchmark of excellence; *exceeding* expectations is damaging and probably even more damaging of trust and confidence than the actions of those lawyers who sometimes fail to meet expectations at all.

That's not to say that expectations should equate to average or ordinary; that is not the point at all. My expectation, for example, of the caterers on my wedding day was exceedingly high, but when I grab a sandwich from a canteen I have a different expectation.

The point is that the lawyer has to actively manage expectations. What does good/great service look like, what does the experience feel like and what does it cost? Then, having set the expectations in the mind of the client, for goodness sake make sure that expectations are met. Articulate value, demonstrate the quality, render your bill, get paid - brilliant!

I once asked a lawyer to describe the service I would get for $500 an hour. When he told me, I told him it was too fancy for my needs and could he please describe the service I would get for $400 an hour. He was completely stumped by the idea. He didn't get the work, but the firm who could describe the $400 an hour service did.

The times we need a rocket scientist are those rare times when we need to fly in the stratosphere; for the most part we can sit in economy in a 747.

I don't want to sound like an old curmudgeon, but it concerns me greatly that we have been fooled into playing pointless performance games which have been made up by PR and HR professionals and we have lost sight of what our clients actually want us to do.

In a nutshell, it is this: "Please don't let me down; be there when you should be, not always when I want you to be (and explain the difference); don't overcharge, deliver on your commitments, work hard, keep me in touch (because I hate surprises) and be good company."

What a great lawyer that would be.

If you strive to exceed expectations, you may be wasting your time and/or my money. Please, please, please just do the job and *meet* my expectations!

11. The Client Conundrum – An essay on the future of legal services

This is a paper about change.

It is not a plea to rally around the latest three-letter acronym from the current most fashionable management school, but an argument for seeing that the world of legal services is adapting rapidly (strategically, operationally and tactically) and that perhaps, just perhaps, what made us successful before might not make us successful going forward.

This paper is also about understanding the elements of service that work today and that will still work tomorrow, so that we do not engage in a headlong rush to change anything and everything without first realising what needs to be preserved.

Current state - it's not so bad, is it?

Law firms are very successful money making machines; business is often hard won and money hard earned, but without doubt law firms are extremely good at generating income. It is sometimes hard to contemplate, therefore, from a distance, why anyone would want to interfere with such a model.

Viewed from a distance, the best firms observe a seemingly centuries old culture of charging for time which has entrenched behaviours passed on from one generation of lawyers to another. Essentially the model is very simple – the income generated from the service delivered has to be around one third more than the cost of delivering the service.

The model is perfectly designed to support the pursuit of remunerated *activity*. Obviously the model does not exclude concepts of quality or cost effectiveness, but it is the case, primarily and dominantly, that remunerated activity is the key to success.

Indeed, while quality has to feature significantly in a successful legal practice, this is measured not in absolute terms related to the deployment of legal expertise, but in *perceptions* of service from the client's perspective and therefore emphasising the importance of client relationship management skills.

Thus the most successful lawyers of recent times have been the so called "rain-makers" – those gods of the profession who could not only develop great swathes of remunerated activity, but who could at the same time make each of their clients feel that they are getting personalised attention.

When framed in these terms, this model it is hard to criticise; and a great many men (and some women) have become wealthy as a result of it.

In summary, the most successful law firms have understood four fundamental truths:

- People buy from people and, however grand the edifice, in the end business is given to those whom we trust to do a good job.

- Service delivery matters more than the quality of activity, because no one but those directly involved knows differently.

- Value is in the eye of the beholder and not intrinsically related to the deal or transaction or matter.

- Activity, activity, activity!

Current state - seeds of doubt:

Over the last few years, however, clients have begun to comment on what might be described as an institutional imbalance in the relationship between law firm and in-house team:

- The in-house team's bargaining power is diminished the closer a crisis looms or the more comfortable a law firm feels with the regularity of activity and the absence of close scrutiny.

- All the likely law firms move at a similar pace, to a similar beat – so nothing truly radical happens in isolation. This creates an almost false loyalty based on an assumption that there is little point shifting activity from one law firm to another because all the main players are so similar.

- In-house teams do not yet feel confident that new charging models (which move away from hourly rates) will make a significant difference to the overall cost of the activity – reasoning that the law firms will make their money one way or another.

However, these seeds of doubt have not been, so far, enough to shift momentum for change. Clearly the pull of the status quo has been so much stronger than the push for possible change.

As a result there has not been a discernible drive for a "new normal", and points of differentiation between law firms are observed on a micro, not a macro, level. This situation is a potential vulnerability for firms, but until now has worked to their advantage, provided firms keep winning a reasonable share of new business.

But our conclusion is that the push for change (the seeds of doubt we have described notwithstanding) has been mostly held back by the failure of clients to be more efficient in their own operations.

If this were to change, if in-house teams become as efficient as they should, then the model is very vulnerable from the firm's perspective.

It is therefore now a fascinating time to observe this transition.

Current state - the client's failure:

To be clear about the issues being described, let us first look at what LBC Wise Counsel has identified as the client side inefficiency, because any efficiency improvement potentially significantly threatens the law firm "current state" model.

In-house teams do not routinely insist on verifiable performance metrics and often lack even rudimentary technology and IT support from their colleagues in the business.

Clients do not routinely allow law firms to build significant and varied contacts beyond the in-house legal team, thus creating a natural bottleneck for instruction and advice.

- Clients occasionally fail to provide sufficient instruction and have insufficient clarity around objectives and goals.

- Errors are then sometimes repeated.

- Clients are often too soft on "project creep".

- In our view, in-house teams will sometimes avoid challenging law firm inefficiency for fear of exposing the issues in question to the scrutiny of others.

- Clients value good service and, if the service ethic is obvious, then any inherent inefficiency of process is more acceptable.

- Many clients do not even know how much work they outsource, at what cost and for what value; this doesn't encourage systematic review.

- Clients have a low expectation of excellence in law firm process management.

- Clients have a high expectation that costs will be significant.

In short, the current state model, allied to client inefficiency, has been a quite brilliant vehicle for generating vast amounts of activity, most of which is paid for on a time-charged basis and not on outcomes delivered.

Ironically, there is perhaps a very good argument that lawyers should not be lambasted for their lack of organisational or managerial insight; instead lawyers should be seen as paragons of commercial virtue, able to make millions from a process and a methodology that was lost to other industries and sectors decades ago!!!

Surely, however, any significant improvement in client side efficiency will put pressure on the current state model and, from our observations of the in-house sector, we believe significant change is indeed under way.

In our judgement we are already moving inexorably towards a new future state.

A new future state?

There are two fundamental reasons to believe that the model will change and change dramatically:

- First, as described above, the improving efficiency of in-house legal teams is encouraging them to demand a change to the current state (more on this shortly).

- Second, and potentially seismically, the regulatory model is about to change as well. I will explore this issue first in the next section of this paper.

Future state - regulatory model change:

The regulatory model will undoubtedly change.

The Legal Services Act is now law and the competitive environment for legal services providers will look very different in perhaps as little as five years time. Perhaps as soon as 2010 new legal entities will be able to seek authorisation to provide legal services and by 2012 the world will be different – but how different?

Henry Ford is reputed to have said that before the automobile had been invented, if you had asked travellers what they would have wanted most to make travel a better experience, they would have said "faster horses".

Seeing into the future for legal services and the legal profession is similarly constraining. We can all have a vague, speculative thought about legal services becoming "quicker, easier, cheaper…" Most of us have bought into this theory already.

For example, thanks to (1) email, (2) document compilation and (3) mobile communications we have made our work a lot, lot quicker. In addition IT for document and case management systems has also made our work a little easier (at least we can handle more complex work more easily) and, as a result of competition for work and talent (combined with the revolution in technology generally), unit costs for most legal services are now cheaper too.

All well and good, but all of this looks more like faster horses than new-fangled automobiles. Where and when will be the step-change, the Henry Ford moment of unleashing a new phenomenon on the profession and their clients?

In my judgement the wider horizon for legal services will change in five fundamental ways:

- Virtual courtrooms providing 24/7 justice
- Corporately sponsored/franchised retail outlets for legal advice, "Lex-savers"
- Broadband document assembly
- Compulsory mediation for dispute resolution
- Intelligent commerce – the Sat-Nav lawyer

Virtual Courtrooms:

The extraordinary waste of the civil and criminal justice systems is the 18th century approach to list management, the lack of project management discipline and the lack of physical availability of judges and space.

The courtrooms of the future will see lawyers, judges and witnesses joined together in a virtual world that is not dependent on everyone being physically co-located at the same time. Representations, arguments and witness examination can be given in downloaded "pod hearings" for judges to ponder at any time of the day or night. Similar (perhaps) to video gaming technology, point and counterpoint can be made without recourse to panelled chambers, but will instead inhabit a world of pixelated images.

"LexSavers R Us":

Thirty years ago nearly every High Street in England had a family-run butcher, optician and pharmacy. Now the supermarkets sell most of the meat and poultry, while the pharmacies and opticians are owned not by families, but by multi-national retail chain stores.

The traditional law firm model of a few partners owning the business and each firm inventing its own brand, marketing, technology solutions etc. will die.

Welcome to the world of franchised law; centralised technology, HR management, marketing and service standards. Welcome to the "have a nice day" culture of up-selling, free gifts with kiddies' advice packs and "buy one, get one free" deals. The owner-managers of today will hate it, but the punter will recognise it, understand it and use it. Such accessible legal services will revolutionise the market-place.

Broadband document assembly:

There was a children's toy on the market a year or so back: it asked you 20 questions and then guessed what it was you were thinking about and nine times out of ten it got it right.

It had the programming capacity of a digital watch and had a 90% success rate - that's pretty neat. Now imagine conducting a commercial transaction: let's buy a company - how many questions would that need? 50? 500? 5,000?

Certainly a few, but probably not many more than would occupy one tenth of the space on one CD. Let's make this a bit more interactive - let's have a virtual lawyer on my desktop that I can interrogate; I suspect that within an hour I can give enough information for my e-lawyer to have compiled most if not all my documents. Then we simply email this to a call centre to get the deal checked over and the very next day I am presented with a suite of documents for signing.

That will be $100 plus tax, please sir. Thank you.

Compulsory mediation:

What is the point of litigation?

It is expensive, slow, cumbersome and brutal. It destroys rather than creates and teaches us only that, if you have enough money, you can win most things. And typically litigation is not about truth or justice; it is about which party can lay its hands on the best evidence and present it better than the other side.

Mediation in civil tort, contract and family issues should be compulsory – no exceptions, because in my future world someone will realise that a no worse result will be achieved, more quickly, less expensively and less destructively, by making disputing parties sit down, discuss their differences and agree a compromise, or have one imposed on them.

When I was a young lawyer, my chief executive demanded I write all my reports on no more than one side of A4. It was a harsh regime, but it focused the mind and it worked. By analogy no mediation should last more than a week and no report should be more than one side of A4!!!

As strap lines are in vogue, try this one, "Get to the point, stick to the point and don't be a smartarse".

The Sat-Nav lawyer:

Everything we do today is governed by regulation: health and safety, employment, anti-discrimination, export, import, revenue, sale of goods, contract etc. etc. etc..

Imagine how useful it would be if we could carry a lawyer around with us at all times.

Even just a few years ago satellite navigation systems were for ballistic missiles or round-the-world sailors; now every salesman, delivery driver and school-run 4x4 has a Sat-Nav system stuck to the dashboard calmly advising us to take the next left turn.

How long before we have the Sat-Nav equivalent in legal services? We set a destination "to employ X on a one year contract" and are told "Please wait a moment while the Sat-Nav lawyer calculates the route" and then, for the next few hours or days or weeks, we respond to the directions given and the Sat-Nav lawyer responds to how we interpret the directions given.

So, these are my five predictions for the next five years: just five, and I am sure that any one of us could think of five more and five more again.

None of these five areas of significant change requires a traditional law firm model; but they will require a very

significant investment in five key areas if law firms are
going to compete in the new market place:

- There will be a very significant investment in building
  and maintaining legal content.

- Different channels for delivery of advice and
  guidance will follow, with less emphasis on the office
  environment and much more emphasis on virtual
  environments and "Sky+" type storage and retrieval.

- Making legal content accessible to non-lawyers will
  be an imperative.

- Creating a brand identity, then maximising brand
  awareness and finally promoting differentiation
  from competitors will require a sophisticated and
  expensive approach to marketing.

- Recruiting entrepreneurial executive talent capable
  of implementing the strategic and operational
  disciplines necessary for success will also be key.

*Some of the thoughts I have set down may seem fanciful,
but the only point I want to emphasise is that the creation
of alternative business entities, funded independently,
with different skills deployed in increasingly imaginative
ways, will result in genuinely entrepreneurial legal
services.*

As a result, points of differentiation between providers
will be on a macro, not micro, level.

Future state - the client side demand for change:

Crucially, however, while I am predicting the most
significant revolution ever in legal services as a result
of regulatory change, it is clear that client attitudes are
already changing.

For a start, even those holding the most relaxed,
optimistic view for benign consequences of change would
concede that the sort of client-side inefficiency we have
previously observed may not be a predictable trend for
the future.

However, much more than this, we believe there are very significant signs of change. For example there is much evidence of increasing sophistication in panel set up.

- In 2007 BOC Linde and Tyco broke new ground with solus appointments on a pan European and even global basis. Also in 2007/8 Severn Trent plc revamped its panel in favour of a single commercial law firm appointment.

- Also in 2007 LBC Wise Counsel advised twenty-two different General Counsel on aspects of panel management and panel review, nine so far in 2008. Process is more evident, metrics feature and articulated value-add is now the norm.

In addition the rise and rise of the procurement professional will not abate. The only likely change we see here is that it will force further rigour on the part of in-house teams (a good thing). In this environment law firms are striving to demonstrate points of differentiation (not sameness) and the more clients push law firms to demonstrate difference, the more law firms have to identify values and activities which are indicative of new thinking around leadership, value and value-add.

We are also witnessing evidence (at last!) of how value is articulated against firmer metrics. If this continues, we predict that law firm "investment" in client relationships might have to become a real cost and not just an opportunity cost. For example, setting up a client extranet to host a few PowerPoint slides will not do; we now expect law firms to commit real resource to developing a bespoke tool of genuine and lasting use.

By way of analogy, when large catering companies win exclusive event management contracts, the capital cost of fitting out kitchens is their cost, not the client's. For law firms, if the client wants £50,000 of IT support to invest in a document management system, the firm might just have to play the game, or walk away from the gig.

These changes are linked to observable trends in the discipline and structure of in-house teams. Indeed LBC

Wise Counsel is responsible for advocating much of the change we believe is now taking place.

The in-house team's new model role:

For many in-house teams activity is managed on informal priorities (who shouts loudest) and nearly always the team is under-resourced to meet the scale of potential demand. The crisis management ethic abounds with teams generally making a good job of rather inefficient time management, resource deployment and prioritisation techniques.

In part, we believe, this is a factor of moving from a law firm environment where "activity" is king, to an in-house environment where "value-add" is far more important. The failure to adjust easily is then exacerbated by what is often an under-resourced environment, where IT support is limited, infrastructure investment limited and resilience across the team also limited.

Nevertheless, the attitude of many General Counsel that might once have been encapsulated in phrases such as "We are too busy to be worried about metrics" is definitely changing and a far more balanced approach is finding favour. In LBC Wise Counsel we have observed something that we call

"The Rule of 4":

In "The Rule of 4" there are four reasons to employ in-house lawyers, four key attributes of an in-house legal team and four key activities comprising the signature profile of excellence in in-house legal services.

We use the Rule of 4 as a consulting template and in many of our workshops.

By developing policies and metrics that support the Rule of 4, in-house teams are stepping away from crisis management and into a more thoughtful deployment of resource to manage risk.

Four reasons to employ an in-house lawyer by which we can devise truly relevant performance metrics:

1. Cost effectiveness

2. Accessibility

3. Knowledge of the client

4. Expert outsourcing

Four key attributes of an in-house team defining the skills that must prevail:

1. Deployment of legal expertise

2. Leveraging knowledge of the client

3. Relationship management

4. Expert prioritisation

Four key activities comprising the signature profile of excellence in in-house legal services and fundamentally the template for success:

1. Meeting known legal need

2. Identifying unknown legal need

3. Wider legal risk awareness

4. Transfer of legal know-how to the business

A confluence of ideas - a challenge of timing, not concept:

In our judgement the rapidly approaching change in the regulatory environment will ignite a raft of innovation and entrepreneurialism that will impact on all legal services providers. It doesn't mean that every law firm has to change everything, but it probably means that every law firm will change something.

Consider, for example, the possible impact on:

- Your recruitment policies – competing with new providers offering "lifestyle" as well as intellectual stimulation.

- Investment in technology – where strategic partnership and joint ventures will make anything spent today look like pennies.

- Investment in delivery channels – downloadable, interactive, bespoke, client driven.

- Publishing – content providers are key players; can you leverage your content?

- Consultancy services – can you move to a defined proactive risk support, training and publishing model?

In addition the pressure to be innovative will drive still harder points of differentiation rather than points of sameness. This in turn feeds the growing sophistication of the in-house teams in the way they select and manage their panels. Again this does not have to signal revolution necessarily, but in a competitive race, coming a close second might mean losing everything - a fact that should be incentive enough for firms to invest so much more energy in client retention, articulating value, delivering value-add etc..

The implications of change on the relationships of the future:

We draw the following conclusions to suggest the strategic direction for relationship development between law firms and in-house teams. We talk about relationship development (as opposed to relationship management) because we believe this will become an even more important activity for all law firms. Each and every relationship will have to be developed and not just "managed".

- Panels will become the standard. Ad hoc arrangements will be seen as eccentric and inefficient.

- Established panels will get smaller. In our judgement managing any more than three to five firms is unworkable, even where volumes are very significant. Law firms will lose more pitches, but, when they win, they will win big

- Client retention will be the key strategic driver and value will be articulated at every contact point.

- There will be a trend towards "solus" appointments, but it won't suit everyone.

- Metrics which show the value of the relationship will be crucial; sophisticated work/value reporting will be routine.

- Value-add initiatives will be real, expensive and a long term commitment

The implications of regulatory change:

This is really too hard to predict, but we believe some ideas feel more resonant than others. For example:

- Legal content publishers and technology companies will be the strategic allies of the law firms. We do not believe law firms will innovate sufficiently from their own resources. In fact, we think it is likely that publishers will become even more significant employers of legal services professionals.

- As mentioned earlier, investment in technology will be fundamental and this in turn will lead to new delivery channels.

- Lawyers are less important in this paradigm

- Unit costs will reduce, the trend will be for further commoditisation

- Law firms that embrace change will thrive; the law firms that do not...

It is indeed a fascinating time. The Client Conundrum, once resolved, will change our profession for ever.

12. Change and Leadership – the essential start-up kit

"Change" is more than a business school process. We must shape the discussion, influence, challenge, adhere to values and inspire. Walk around any bookstore and sooner or later you will come across literally hundreds of books on leadership, on change, on transformation, on process improvement, on personal improvement, on team development - shelf after shelf after shelf after shelf. If the weight of this literary contribution is anything to go by, is it any wonder that "Change" and "Leadership" sound like a subjects done to death?

So let me state my case at the outset - I am *not* going to make an argument for some new-fangled process; there will be neither trite slogans nor clever acronyms. I am not going to pretend to have an insight beyond that which we could all bring and I am not going to recommend anything that we will think contrary to our own intuition.

I do, however, link change with leadership and see the two ideas as inexorably tied together. For me, the best change programmes are ones that are both accessible to those involved and affected and achievable as planned. Invariably the qualities of leadership involved are not clichéd and stereotypical, but are largely concerned with influencing and communicating thoughtfully.

I am also writing this article, if I am honest, to present my vision of change and leadership as an antidote to the trite, overly simplistic and the falsely evangelical.

Maybe it is because I am a natural sceptic, but I have always disliked unfeasibly toned fitness gurus telling me that if I wobble around on an over large beach ball it will give me "abs" like theirs. I distrust the autobiographical books by retired CEOs that tell me to "think success" to make the difference. I also object strongly to legions of sharp-suited teenagers strolling around established businesses making life-changing decisions for hard-working people when they themselves haven't yet figured out that in the real world work is not organised into semesters!

I object, basically, to the "quick fix" and to anyone with an attitude that suggests that anything tried and trusted is inadequate unless given a makeover of some description. I think my first serious life-lesson on this subject occurred when I moved from one big job to another about ten years ago. In the one company I was considered a star performer, someone at the top of his game making an important contribution. I was surrounded by talent and the company was a great success. I then moved to a company that was much less successful; in fact it was badly broken as a business and eventually had to be sold or it would have failed completely.

It made me realise two things:

- First, I was not as good as I thought I was!

- Second, my new colleagues were just as talented, just as committed, just as capable of success as my former colleagues, but they had not had a chance to show what they were capable of delivering.

The lesson for me was very powerful; I learnt that success is only partly due to the talent pool - it is an important part, but probably less important than the quality of leadership and the way our people are organised to allow them to flourish. It also convinced me that any team and any company already has the talent, the intelligence and the ability to effect changes that will make that team or company much more successful. No books, no gurus, no acronyms required; we have the talent within all of us already; so how can we lead our teams to bring about lasting and effective change relying on *our* talent.

The issues we will have to address will vary, but in my judgement it is how we begin our work that determines how successful we will be. Leading change is one of the hardest things we will ever do, but understanding our role as leaders and understanding how this impacts on the way we plan for change is fundamental to the success of any project.

The bullet points below do not present some wonderfully illuminating insight: this is practical stuff, but these are the issues we must all address. This is the crucial work; this is where we lay the foundations for future success:

What are the obstacles to change and how can you anticipate better what they will be? In this regard it is a necessity to brainstorm and consult, engage and listen. Plan to succeed and plan to have contingency as well. The idea for change is the easy bit, but seeing the interplay between competing priorities, dependencies and resources is the art.

- How will influencing and relationship management sit at the centre of all you are planning? What perceptions must you manage, what expectations have been set? Whom do you need to win round, who needs incentivising and whom do you need to confront?

- How should you lead debate when you do not control participants or outcomes? Influencing others is a key skill and you will need to identify all the interests in play.

- What are the requirements for engagement and how can you encourage behaviours supportive of your agenda? This is an ongoing commitment from any leader. Communication is never "accomplished"; at best it is only ever "so far so good"!

- What will be the signature profile of a successful outcome? Can you describe successful outcomes in different ways to appeal to different interests? Can you choreograph quick wins and plan for a communication strategy around outcomes?

- What are the essential disciplines for increasing the probability of success? Who do you need on the team and why/when will they join you? Invest in success; don't just start a project and hope for the best.

Already I am guilty of oversimplification, but I hope you will see this as just a start. These are the practical, pragmatic issues you need to address and while the wisdom of ancient Chinese philosophers may not be something we should dwell on for too long, to end this brief explanation I will refer to the words of Confucius who said:

"Tell me and I'll forget. Show me and I'll remember. Involve me and I'll understand."

As a template for leading and effecting change, it is not a bad place to pin our colours. It is just a beginning, but starting well is how we can best assure a successful finish.

13. Does size matter so much?

There is much talk around the world of consolidation in legal services; the globalisation strategies of some high profile law firms is mimicked by firms in individual countries and across regions seeking to grow through their own merger strategies. But while there is an obvious argument that supports larger full-service law firms with a significant regional footprint, is this the best way for the legal services market to evolve?

I pose the question fully aware that some who have heard me speak before on this subject, advocating in particular change to meet client demand for more services, more depth, more coverage etc., will perhaps think I am contradicting myself.

I have said many times, because I have seen it with my own eyes, that there is a deepening and fast moving trend for corporate clients to reduce the number of different firms they use and to want more from the firms they choose.

But I do not advocate merger as a panacea to meet the demands of such clients – big is not always beautiful.

In my view the evolution of legal services will create change in two distinct and diverging directions; each will drive innovation, each will take advantage of the entrepreneurialism of younger leaders and each will seek strategic alliances in sectors such as publishing and information technology.

On the one hand, size matters and indisputably so.

One-off mega deals often go to the largest firms, but, this aside, many corporate clients are setting up their law firm panels not just to provide transactional legal services, but to help manage legal risk across disciplines and across borders. Panels must be vehicles in part for information management and risk management and in part to help train, develop and embed best practice in creative, pre-emptive and pro-active ways.

Clients also know that to demand so much means that law firms will expect long term relationships that are not just profitable, but which also carry a predictable expectation of significant volumes of activity as well. This in turn must result in smaller panels, with fewer, larger firms offering great relationship and business development expertise.

In short, therefore, firms of a certain size that aspire to be engaged by such clients must see that merger is their best (only?) opportunity to survive and thrive.

But at the same time, some large corporate clients who are less dependent on legal services, not to mention the huge swathe of smaller clients with less legal work anyway, still want and need great legal services, and they have a different world view.

Their perspective is not to have the management challenge of a fixed panel of uber firms, but to look for something more aligned to their needs - perhaps driven by the complexity and diversity of their activity; or perhaps because their work is ad hoc and unpredictable; or perhaps because in the end they are driven by value more than by value-add.

For these clients the huge beasts of the legal jungle will look over-hyped, over-bearing and clunky. The largest firms that need to roam on a national, regional, even global basis to feed the legions of staff they employ in their cathedrals to the great god of the billable hour, will not have the time or the appetite to deploy their resources for clients who cannot predict volume or even type of activity.

So, in very simplistic terms, we are heading for a significant divergence in law firm strategies:

- First, those firms that compete for pan-regional, volume-predictable activity, seeking clients from whom they can suck great chunks of work.

- Second, the firms that seek to provide a bespoke legal service, tailored to need, for a reasonable fee.

In the second camp, speciality will be prized, as will value for money, as will sector know-how. But this is not going to be a safe haven for the firms that lose out on the merger/growth curve; this alternative route to success is not a default position.

The firms that succeed will be equally entrepreneurial - for example in their recruitment policies, in the way they incentivise and retain staff, in their flexibility to client needs, in the nimbleness and cleverness of their solutions, in their deployment of information technologies and in the way they build and sustain brand and reputation.

The losers - and there will be losers - will be the law firms that decide they can "wait and see", whose strategy is based on hope and not conviction.

In the UK right now many of the best (some also of the biggest) law firms are considering how to respond to the Legal Services Act 2007, a piece of legislation that offers the opportunity for non-lawyer owners in law firms and alternative business structures. For the first time success may be determined not by the quality of the lawyers (although this is obviously still a key component), but by the quality of the strategy.

The UK for now might be considered a special case, but the ideas won't be retained within the UK and the ripple effect of entrepreneurial legal services and the increasing sophistication of the client purchasing decision will drive change across jurisdictions.

To the old certainties (death and taxes) add a third, change. Legal services are going to change – structurally firms will need to move away from the old partnership models to become more adaptable to new opportunities, publishers of legal know-how are going to be as important for many firms as the lawyers they retain; technology, offering new channels of access and delivery, will open new markets. There is so much to consider and in reality not that much time to get it right.

So, does size matter? You bet; it is a clear differentiator and a cogent response to the market trends, but it is not the only strategy in town.

14. A "crunch"... The collective noun for failed bankers

At the time of writing this article I am pleased to confirm that the world has not ended.

It is an important point to make; I would not want to waste my time if it had ended. I will also be an optimist and assume, for now, that the world will not have ended by the time you read these words.

Yet to listen to the constant reporting of the banking crisis in the press, on television, on the radio and across the internet, one would assume that the world was close to imploding. A pinstriped induced Armageddon

Okay...clearly it is a weird time.

A time when The United States government can find $700bn (that's *seven...hundred...billion*...dollars) to underwrite so called "toxic" loans, yet continues to fail miserably to look after its own most vulnerable citizens who cannot access even basic healthcare.

A time when banks that have existed for 150 years, that employ tens of thousands of people and have millions of customers can merge literally overnight, yet tax payers have paid billions of Euros a year, for years, to keep bureaucrats in Brussels regulating deals and preventing mergers taking place that do not fit their competition policies

A time when world leaders can posture about wars they fight in far away countries that harbour radicalised young men and women, but where a few people much closer to home, radicalised by greed, can cripple nations without a bullet or a bomb in sight.

The crisis in banking will be remembered for many things, but not the end of the world. The crisis in banking will be remembered, I hope, as the time ordinary citizens saw their leaders in a different light and began to demand a different type of leadership.

Could we see elected politicians who recognise that they are in power to serve their fellow citizens - not protected interests, globalising business executives, or self-serving self-perpetuating governmental institutions?

When one government can bail out Wall Street at a cost of $700bn, no government will ever again be able to say they cannot afford to look after the poor, the sick and the infirm and be believed. It is just a question of relative priority and, crucially, of ethics.

When your local hospital is threatened with closure, politicians are used to saying that restructuring local healthcare means hard decisions have to be taken: will this be acceptable now? When natural disasters strike, world leaders are used to authorising limited aid and relying on charities to take up the demand: will this be acceptable now? When politicians buy arms instead of HIV drugs, will this be acceptable now?

How much good would $700bn do in our world if it weren't spent on bankers?

And because it is a question of priorities and ethics, let's see our lawyers step up to the mark and be counted.

The legal press in recent weeks has reported the credit crunch in one of two ways – how many lawyers are losing their jobs in big city firms and, conversely, which firms are working on the mega deals arising from the restructuring of the banking sector. As an exercise in journalistic merit, it lacks any insight and is entirely facile.

I believe the challenge and opportunity for the legal profession is much, much greater; it is nothing less than to be part of the informal regulatory regime for capitalism.

In future in-house legal teams should consider it to be part of their brief to actively manage reputational risk, to be the keeper of the corporate conscience, to place constraints on sales targets that compromise appropriate risk taking.

In conversation many in-house lawyers would say they already consider this to be part of their role in any event, but in the light of the humiliation of banks around the world, this must now become a practical reality, not just nice words in theory.

I wonder if individual shareholders might even start to look at in-house lawyers and put on them a specific duty to look after their interests. Perhaps this simply makes explicit that which is already the case.

And for law firms instructed by their major corporate clients, a duty perhaps to advise on the context as well as the detail. In future when deals are proposed, it shouldn't be enough for lawyers to say that it "can be done"; perhaps now there should be a responsibility to say whether it "should be done". And again shareholders holding advisers to account: no good to say, "Yes, it was legal"; the question will be, "But was it also the right thing to do?"

It sounds vague, difficult and potentially dangerous, but lawyers have always put themselves in positions to challenge overbearing and dominant forces, whether state or business, to represent the best interests of those without the same resources to protect themselves.

Those minority interests - be they employees, consumers or citizen tax payers -   now need the legal profession to assert and uphold ethical business practices.

Not all lawyers will relish the challenge, but if the world of business is going to progress from the utter folly and mess made by our bankers, it will not be iron-fisted government appointed regulators who make it happen (after all until now they were part of the problem, not the solution); it will be trusted advisers, close to the deals, close to the decision makers, who can guide, influence and cajole appropriate behaviours and appropriate risk taking.

For many years I have encouraged lawyers to be more businesslike in their approach – adaptable to change, embracing of new technologies etc., but I am a passionate believer in the vocational imperative of what being a lawyer means.

Lawyers must now step up and be players in this new world; not just facilitators, not just clever wordsmiths, not just attack dogs for executive talent, but independently minded guardians of what is acceptable business practice.

Perhaps, after all, some good will come of all this nonsense.

15. One prick to burst a bubble

The last few months have been awful.

Whatever your political leaning, whatever your own perspective on how things should have been and how they should be, we are all clearly experiencing the global economy having a major tantrum; toys thrown out of the pram with gusto.

Banks are tumbling, resembling castles made from cards rather than the mighty edifices we all thought they were; and easy finance, as a result, is no longer a lubricant in the economy's engine, but might as well be sand. Companies are struggling to plan for the year ahead, workers are being laid off, savers don't know where to put their money and consumers are not spending anything like enough to bring confidence back into the markets.

It is as if we have all caught a sort of global flu bug and all we can do is go to bed for a while and feel sorry for ourselves.

In the midst of this whirlwind of bad news and concern law firms are clearly not immune. It is, however, interesting to see that the legal press mostly reports the impact on lawyers in one of two ways; either the fact of law firms being appointed to run the latest big banking merger/rescue deals (an "ill wind" perhaps) or the fact that some law firms are having to reduce headcount in the face of the economic slowdown.

However, as yet, I have not seen anything written about how law firms should be responding to clients in this new environment.

I once wrote that it was all very well for law firms to make a lot of money when the economy was with them, but that it only takes one prick to burst a bubble. Perhaps unkindly I suggested that the City of London was not prick-free and we should therefore imagine that the bubble would burst. But cheap shots are easy; the question remains, what should be done?

I think law firms of whatever size or complexity have to do three things internally and three things externally:

Actions law firms should take internally:

1. First, engage with every member of the team. What can we each of us do that will help us be more alive to the necessity to run our business a little more tightly? Not arbitrary cuts that always seem to be handed down from on high by the people who have taken the biggest salaries, but thoughtful and meaningful engagement. The fact that budgets are threatened is not going to be a surprise to anyone (we all understand that), but what grates is when decisions are taken too far away from the point of impact. Engage, involve and share.

2. Second, make sure your intelligence about clients is up-to-date and, again, shared within the firm. More than ever now we should be looking at clients as being "of the firm", not to be jealously guarded by relationship partners fearful of their clients suffering a stampede of well-intentioned but inept cross-selling opportunities. The requirement is to make sure that clients feel supported and appreciated, but before this point the firm has to have a forensic appreciation of how the clients operate, their threats and their opportunities and then how those threats and opportunities translate into threats and opportunities for the law firm.

3. Third, law firms have got to be so much more inventive now. This isn't something you can just turn on; it is about encouraging a level of debate and thoughtfulness from the junior ranks up. If the prevailing climate is fearful, invention is not what you get. Fear suffocates invention and chokes opportunity. This therefore is a leadership challenge and, if the law firm's leadership can encourage invention, there are three areas to focus on:

- Be more inventive around fees (are hourly rates still a feasible charging method when every client is trying to have budgetary certainty?), but consider as well how the firm can be aligned to cashflow in their clients. It is now about financial planning and an ability to have adult conversations about risk and reward.

- Be more inventive around ancillary support, finding ways to embed the firm within the client – for example with secondees, knowledge management and risk management.

- Finally be more inventive around packaging services so that the communication of what the law firm does is not centred on subject specialism, but around value-add. Clients don't want to buy litigation, but they might buy risk reduction consultancy if the price is right and the value well articulated.

Having focused on three things law firms should do internally, what are the three things law firms should do externally?

This is not the time to mess up with any of your current contacts and everyone has a part to play. Reception staff who meet and greet clients, assistants who answer the phone and of course lawyers working directly with contacts have got to be at the very top of their game. Treat every client well, return calls, be punctual, don't over-elaborate, stay on budget, etc. etc. Just do it as well as you possibly can!

- Be as thoughtful as you can around supporting clients in need and be alive to their concerns so that you do not appear to profit from their misfortune. It is a cliché to talk of "sharing pain", but what impact do you think it would have if the firm wrote to an important client and unilaterally offered to reduce legal bills by 10% for a period of 6 months as a gesture of goodwill in these straitened times? In my presentations and workshops I regularly encourage lawyers to be "literally thoughtful". What can you do that will make a difference to your contacts?

- Finally, don't look desperate! Recently I have heard some partners almost plead for work and others who have been gratuitously critical of other firms in a bid to talk up their credentials. Most clients are turned-off by this sort of behaviour. In a crisis (and it is a crisis for many) there is always credit to be won for behaving well. Don't let your standards slip.

I am not sure every cloud will have a silver lining and I am not sure every silver lining will be enough to preserve every job, but there is still opportunity in adversity and those who seize the opportunities will survive and be all the stronger for it.

16. Open Source Law?

There is a phenomenon in the world of systems development and software that might just have the most enormous impact on the future of legal services.

As we all know, lots of software is proprietary, but much more is known as open source code. Microsoft has been the arch proponent of the proprietary model, jealously guarding its source code and fiercely antagonistic to anyone seeking to use it without permission. Yet there are millions of applications that use code that was freely given away to help generate solutions and to facilitate invention. The internet itself is perhaps the best and most widely used example of the open source model.

Open source code is royalty free and available for programmers to use to enhance, in essence, the consumer's experience. It is as if the code itself does not have an intrinsic value; its value is realised only when the code is used within an application which is then used in a process or system by a consumer.

It is possible for philanthropic authors everywhere to be influential (if not always remunerated) beyond imagining if their code is picked up and widely used. It has been a subject that has fascinated me for some time because I see an analogy in legal services that carries both an enormous opportunity and an enormous threat.

What if all legal knowledge was to be treated as if it were open source code?

Law firms, instead of jealously guarding their precedents and their know-how, would simply make it available to anyone who wanted to use it.

In the USA the Massachusetts Institute of Technology (MIT), one of the most prestigious seats of learning in the world, now publishes in their entirety all its lecturers' notes for anyone to use one year after the courses are delivered.

What a brilliant statement of self confidence, what a wonderful resource for those interested in the subjects concerned and what a great way to share understanding and help develop new ideas.

The analogy with legal know-how might not be exact, but it has a resonance with what I see as the two key drivers of value in legal services - and neither is about the intrinsic value of legal knowledge.

I believe only two things will be valuable going forward:

1. The quality of relationships managed and developed by lawyers.

2. Control over the means of distribution.

In other words, either lawyers will be remunerated because they have great relationships with the clients who use them and it will be the added value that comes from the quality of those relationships that is worth paying for or lawyers will control how legal knowledge can be disseminated and the means of distribution will be what creates the value.

In the first scenario, the client will appreciate the bespoke solution, tailored, relevant and contextualised; it is a premium rate service built on a trusted adviser status and delivers value through an intimate understanding of interests, not through any intrinsic value in the legal know-how itself. It will be about value enhancement and relationship development and will probably be expensive. For the relationship to be valued then, law firms are going to need the equivalent of concierge services, relationship managers who are simply brilliant at relationship management, not lawyers bullied into trying to cross-sell on behalf of partners they hardly know.

In the second scenario, legal know-how has been commoditised and packaged with any bespoke angle removed (or left only to a drop-down menu); it is probably a partial solution, but its accessibility, brand credentials and customer feedback will sell it. It is the "pile 'em high, sell 'em cheap" solution and in this case value for the provider will come from owning the franchise, the website, the affinity relationship or the publisher. Hardly any value will be attributed to the quality of the legal know-how, but enormous value will flow to those who control the means of distribution.

Almost everything that lawyers do today will be pushed to one of these two extreme categorisations and virtually nothing will fall between the two; and if you buy into that analysis and into these two models, then there are some hard and quick decisions to take going forward.

Most law firms will need a joint venture partner for the second scenario to work for them and only a few joint venture partners are available currently who will do this well.

In my opinion we are now only a matter of months away from lawyers selling products through EBay, reverse auctions, on free discs inside magazines and as add-ons to insurance products sold in supermarkets and on price comparison websites (indeed I am sure some people reading this article will tell me that it is already happening).

I do not, however, see these as doomsday events that will only result in the killing of hapless law firms for the sake of progress; but I do think that as the world around us changes, so must legal services adapt to new expectations and new opportunities.

The music industry is still coming to terms with the fact that singers and songwriters will not always be paid because they can sing or write songs. Lawyers must now face a similar challenge - no longer paid for knowing the law, but paid because they are brilliant at managing complex relationships for value, or paid because they have the means to disseminate information in ways that people want to buy.

Up selling is only an ad break away!

And if that means that entrepreneurial talent can help us all deliver more value, then that is something we have to explore; given the deregulation of the market, surely it is better for lawyers to be designers and architects in this brave new world than to be merely the facilities management?

17. Lessons to learn and things to do

Some very notable minds down the ages have suggested that "the only thing we learn from history is that we do not learn from history". At this time particularly this seems a rather unhelpful thought on which to dwell; even if we do not learn from history, it is surely tempting nonetheless to wonder how the flying fig tree did we ever end up where we are today!

Clearly these are not good times; markets have been in meltdown, banks are still in disarray, manufacturing seems to be teetering on the brink of a major recession and even law firms are laying off hundreds of lawyers, while television commentators and journalists are looking for the opportunity to make their careers with national prominence and, no doubt, the odd prestigious award.

These are indeed not good times; some might even think this period is more than a little surreal, but when the emotional dust has settled a little and the bar room economists have given way to those of us left to make the best of things as they still stand, what should we do? What should we do, indeed?

In my view in-house legal teams have now to address ten key issues; but this is not a ten point plan for survival nor is it about "making do" in straitened times. I think it is much more positive than that and many of the issues I cover, in fact, will have resonance whatever the economic climate. That said, we cannot escape the point that, with significant costs being saved, anyone in an in-house role is potentially at some risk. At best we all face the prospect that more has to be managed with less, probably for some time to come.

This is a time, therefore, for thoughtful leadership and the clarity of approach which will stand any team in better shape for the times, hopefully not so far away, when our businesses can be more self-confident and plan for growth.

Nothing in my ten-point plan is about knee-jerk responses to the present economic privations; all the points, I hope, can be considered as part of a careful and balanced approach to managing risk and delivering value.

1. Define the role of the in-house team

No team on the planet can be (or should even try to be) a full service in-house legal function. There will always be work that is outsourced and always legal risk that is, for whatever reason, left unmanaged. When resources are so precious, however, now is the time to define the role. The 2x2 grid below is obviously rudimentary, but we must all carefully consider the definition of work and its categorisation.

Work which is **core** and **urgent**	Work which is **core** and **not urgent**
Work which is **not core** and **urgent**	Work which is **not core** and is **not urgent**

It must be the case that, going forward, in-house legal teams focus on the "core and urgent" work, ensuring that as little non-urgent, non-core work as possible is part and parcel of the daily routine and remembering always that providing a great service is not about pleasing people, but about doing the right things.

2. Develop the strategy for using external lawyers

Some commentators might suggest that now is a great time to drive a bargain on fees. I think that risks being a cheap shot.

If we believe in the quality of relationships, if we want commitment and partnership, then driving down fees may only give short-term gain; it is also potentially destructive of value, of quality and of the long-term investment in strategically significant relationships. It is easy to posture and as an example I read recently how in-house teams should now force change on advisers - how shallow.

It is clear that some change may be appropriate, but not through the arrogant demands of a General Counsel who perceives a chance to drive a hard bargain. Perhaps panels should be rationalised, perhaps using fewer firms makes sense (it might make sense anyway), but now is the time to sit down with your law firms to solve problems together and I suggest you look at three things:

- What does the business need and how much can it afford? Does the cost of outsourcing legal work have to reduce? If it does, then in what areas and by how much? What impact does this have on quality and on risk management?

- What do the law firms need from the relationship? Will they trade some cost reduction for more certainty of volume? Would they be willing to provide a service in a different way to save costs (secondments perhaps)?

- What does the in-house team need from the relationships with law firms? Management information and performance indicators may need to be aligned to efficiency and savings in costs; personal development and CPD might need to be devolved entirely to the law firm.

Dialogue is crucial.

3. Focus on value and value-add, not just cost reduction

Cost reduction can drive many positive things; it can lead to process improvement, it can lead to policy efficiency and it can cut out waste. These are things, however, that should be looked at in the best of times, not just now.

When I look at the question of how to save costs, the first issue to address is to identify those things that the team does that adds value; let's not throw baby out with the bath water. I want to know how aligned the team is to the strategic imperatives and how much good the team does as a result.

The second issue to address is how we can then improve the policy and process around those key value-adding activities. Sooner or later the analysis will reveal those activities that are adding less value. The question then is to determine what consequences flow from ceasing that work. In my experience there is always a rump of work which for often unfathomable reasons the legal team has always done. This work has no other natural home and would be inconvenient if it was stopped, but it doesn't add value.

At this point any decisions will be taken in the context of clarity and progress, given that the in-house team has already:

- Identified its most value-adding activity
- Considered process improvement and policy efficiency around this activity
- Identified the low risk, least valuable work and can now make rational decisions about how this work should be resourced going forward

Again the opportunity is for thoughtful dialogue, not for quick and sometimes harsh cuts.

4. Ensure internal processes are secure

When resources are tight and business pressures build, it is easy for some corners to be cut and for some issues to be considered less robustly. This is a potential risk and it should be thoughtfully managed.

Throughout any business there will be processes and policies that have been developed with support and guidance from the in-house lawyers. Compliance in the widest sense of the word is part and parcel of good business where trading ethically and with regard to local laws is essential, regardless of the macro economic picture.

The challenge for the in-house legal team is to be proactive and thoughtful. My strong steer is for every in-house legal team to launch a process review initiative.

Every team should be announcing that it will immediately undertake a thorough and detailed review of all business critical process and policies to identify appropriate relaxations and other safe changes that can speed process or take out cost. Don't wait to be asked; this is your prerogative and your expertise.

5. Still look for cost savings

All that having been said, the in-house legal team should not be immune from looking for cost savings. I used to have a director who challenged me every year to find five separate savings of just £5,000. You might think that this was hardly worth doing, but the exercise was always worthwhile.

I used to engage the whole team in the pursuit of savings and some of the things we found included renegotiating the vending machine leases, changing the toner supplier, outsourcing our library, renegotiating the value-add elements with law firms, recycling stationery and changing our travel policies.

I know some of this is plain obvious, but the important point is to get the whole legal team engaged across the business. If the lawyers are perceived as ultra cost-conscious and careful with the company's money, it carries enormous weight with bosses and will help you to preserve the important things when you are under scrutiny.

6. Invest in technology

I doubt any team in the current climate will negotiate new spending opportunities, but this is my hobby horse just now.

The absence of meaningful management information in many teams means that it is hard to do the analysis I have suggested earlier. I am not a fan of overblown, expensive kit; I am not a believer in placing administrative burdens on the legal team that do not have real added value, but I do think there are systems on the market that are relatively inexpensive (they can even be rented by the week) and which are easy to implement and which will give vital information to the team.

If the business case can be made that an investment of £x will mean a saving of £x+y, then that case should be made. If the in-house team ducks this issue, then it risks losing out to more capricious decisions, and the lack of transparency will not help anyone.

7. Network like fury

I have to pose a slightly negative thought amid my unrelenting positivity! You may lose your job. And if you don't lose your job, you may find career options are curtailed. I therefore think that, in the maelstrom of furious activity, there should be a small space that is self-serving. We should all be networking like fury. What is your market intelligence like? How many people do you consider reliable contacts? In how many sectors do you have people you could call?

Networking will not necessarily find you a new role, but it will help you evaluate the opportunities for career change and to balance what you have now when other opportunities might present themselves.

Networking, to return to my "glass half-full" tone, will also give you a great chance to sense-check the value of your initiatives to save money or improve efficiency and to swap ideas and information that will help you deliver more value to your business.

8. Align performance indicators to your business needs

It is sometimes possible that the things we value most should be valued less when circumstances change. I remember working with an in-house team that focused so much on ensuring that every single piece of legal advice was routed through the legal team that it didn't realise what a bottleneck the team had become.

It was a very commendable thing that legal risk was so tightly managed and the team could assert that everything the business did was overseen by a lawyer; it was, however, a great shame that the business did not value the service and thought the lawyers to be uncommercial and bureaucratic.

It is the particular responsibility of the General Counsel to lead the debate and test assumptions with senior colleagues. There should be no question marks around the commercial credentials of the lawyers and our business colleagues should see and appreciate that the in-house team is aligned to their objectives too.

9. Continue to offer personal development opportunities

My guess is that, for the next year or more, promotion opportunities will diminish and pay rises may be less generous. In these more difficult times, therefore, ensuring that the personal development of the lawyers in the team is not compromised is a very powerful signal to them that they are still a very valued resource.

Consider for example:

- Short term secondments to law firms

- Short term secondment swaps with other in-house teams

- Spending more time in business areas to learn more about the operational priorities

- Ensuring as much training as possible is sourced through the law firms you use, but not just the typical seminars, something much more bespoke and even tailored to the individual

- Networking though regional lawyer groups (why not start your own?)

- Networking in local business community groups such as regional CBI

10. Deliver and articulate value

My final point is a point for all seasons, but it has never been more important.

Lawyers are not valued because they know lots about laws, rules and regulations. Lawyers are valued because they listen well, empathise and find solutions that are accessible and easy to implement.

Lawyers are valued because they both deliver and articulate value; this mantra must be at the heart of every action and every interaction. I want lawyers through their emails, calls, meetings and reports to exude a sound commercial appreciation of their vital role in the communication and value chain and to know when to intervene and when not to.

Be confident, be proactive, be sensitive and be good. Nothing is certain, but improving the probability of our success is something we all can influence. This is our responsibility and it is one we owe to our businesses, to our colleagues and to ourselves.

18. Managing to lead, because we are all leaders now

The difference between what is a "leader" and what is a "manager" and what is "leadership" and "management" is the stuff of consulting heaven! It is a debate that has spawned thousands of books, articles and workshops...and no doubt there are still careers that will be made for the man or woman who can coin an original bon mot to capture the very essence of the distinction.

As I have never been one to fear to tread boldly where the once uncertain path has already been beaten into a multi-lane highway, here is my take on what leadership means and why, like it or not, we are all in leadership roles:

The phone rings and is answered by the personal assistant; his boss is in an important meeting and he would not normally interrupt her. The call is from his boss's Chairman; an important but not critical message is taken. In this situation should the PA interrupt his boss's meeting?

The PA as manager would take the message and reflect on how his boss would read it. Would she want to be interrupted or not? Depending on how he interprets this question, he will act accordingly.

The PA as leader would ask the Chairman, "She is in a very important meeting just now, but will be finished in an hour. Do you want me to interrupt her or can I get her to call you as soon as she is done?"

In the first instance the PA managed the situation against known norms; in the latter, the PA leads by testing whether the known norms need to move; he then takes the initiative, offers a solution and acts on guidance that he himself has helped to shape.

You are a junior lawyer called into a meeting to represent the law firm with a client who will instruct the firm on an important but not terribly complicated deal. In the meeting everyone is senior to you.

Should you simply introduce yourself and take notes?

As manager, you ask pertinent questions about the deal and take copious notes. The notes are obviously being taken to inform the team and the client will normally reflect that this is a satisfactory way to proceed, but there is a danger that you are perceived as little more than a waiter taking a food order to the kitchen - a conduit without too much value-add.

As leader, you will probe the client about their business, their objectives, their hopes and fears. You will be genuinely interested in what the client does and what the client wants. The same notes are taken for the same purposes, but now you are perceived to be more of a player, an influencer, a champion – a leader.

A bank project to launch a new IT platform for savings accounts is running into the ground; there are delays and budget overruns. You are the in-house lawyer on the project responsible for ensuring that the technical specification is developed and tested so that it meets all the relevant regulatory compliance requirements.

As manager, you have a file of notes and messages clearly delineating that you have done all you could, that any delay is at the door of others and that as soon as the project can be put back on track, you are willing and able to make a full and valuable contribution. In the meantime you have plenty of more productive work to do.

As leader, you will be on the phone to the project team encouraging and challenging everyone to find the bottlenecks and the obstacles, offering to help move things forward and leaving your legal brief behind to support activity in whatever way you can. You, the in-house lawyer as leader, are not a busy-body or the classroom snitch, but someone who through energy, integrity and empathy with people can begin to unblock problems and encourage momentum for the greater benefit of your own responsibilities.

Your eldest daughter, just six years old, is in a school play with a solo verse to sing. You are called into a significant meeting with your Chief Executive which is due to start at 6pm, but if you are not away by 6.15pm you risk missing her sing.

As manager, you probably dislike this situation more than most, but you rationalise that it might be career limiting to miss the CEO's meeting; you might even judge that you could make it up to your daughter, but might not have the chance to make it up to your CEO!

As leader, you phone your Chief Executive and explain that this is one of those very rare occasions when you simply have to be somewhere else. You offer to call in later, to check for voicemail etc. and you confirm that you are content for actions to be designated your responsibility in your absence; you also offer to send someone in your place.

Any Chief Executive worthy of the name will encourage you to see your daughter and be grateful for your frankness and your humanity.

You are asked to attend a networking event to launch a new book on legal best practices. There will be around sixty people at the event and you suspect you know probably two of them.

As manager, you attend the event, but once there you stay in the shadows until you spot the one or two people you know; you then make a beeline for them. You enjoy their company; it is good to catch up after all. Then after an appropriate amount of time (just enough to give the appearance that you have made an effort) you leave. Once home you send a message to your boss on your Blackberry that you have been to the event (thus ensuring your great sacrifice of an evening out late is duly noted).

As leader, you request an attendance list in advance and you consciously note the people who will be there; you look for connections, for common interests and for opportunities to share information. You know this is not the place to ask favours or to overtly sell or proposition, but it is the place to test views, to judge interests and to offer to help others with their concerns and issues. As leader, you don't outstay your welcome, but later you write a few emails to the people you met thanking them for their time.

You are the junior partner in a law firm; the client has now instructed you on three separate deals to review relatively similar, but different, sets of terms and conditions. Each piece of work costs the client $5000, but in your view, for an investment of $8000, the client would be able to develop their own standard terms and conditions and not have to instruct you again.

And you know the answer to this one already.

You see, we are all leaders now.

19. Report on Value

Introduction:

In 2008 the regional events division of LBC Wise Counsel, LBConnect, held a series of regional debates for in-house lawyers on value. Debates took place in Leeds, Manchester, Birmingham, Milton Keynes, Bristol Reading, Fareham and Maidstone - in all nearly twenty different events across the country.

All the events were held under Chatham House rules with an invited audience of in-house lawyers drawn from teams across each participating region and representing a wide cross section of sectors and industries including financial services, the public sector, the university sector, manufacturing, retail, pharmaceuticals, utilities and IT. The size of teams represented also varied considerably and ranged from one team with nearly one hundred fee earners to one with just two lawyers.

The first series of debates considered the value of the in-house team, the second series considered the value of the individual in-house lawyer looking at the qualities and competencies needed to succeed and in the third series participants reviewed the value that can be derived from relationships with law firms.

Series one - The value of the in-house team

The following points represent a snap-shot of opinion from the debates. These points are not grouped or prioritised, but we think they make an interesting overview for the following sections of the report. Later we will examine the threat some of these points represent and also the great opportunity for lawyers to make a lasting and significant impact on their businesses.

- **Different operational models** - Some teams work in a central services model where user departments effectively contract internally with the team on well defined service level agreements. Others work on a model that is a simple "on-demand" service, while other teams are decentralised with lawyers assigned to business teams. All teams, however, are aware that they need credible metrics to support their work.

- **A struggle for metrics** - In all three models there was consensus that while obvious things could be measured (number of matters under management, turnaround time, response times etc.), no one appears to have discovered the performance measures that show genuine value for the work completed by the team.

- **More work, more risk, but often no more resource** - In addition the background context for all teams is one where they are expected to manage more activity, more efficiently and often with no more resource.

- **Concern over unmet legal need** - All teams have identified that they are themselves aware of more legal risk management activity that they would like to develop, but most have so far felt unable to tackle new work because of resourcing issues. Some teams expressed concern that they were in fact unable to give the time to consider "unmet" legal need (let alone manage any new work).

- **The rise of risk managers?** - There is a discernible trend in some teams to separate risk assessment from the legal function's operational role. Some teams have even created a risk manager role.

- **Cost reduction is a key driver** - All teams report more pressure on reducing costs and some concern that, notwithstanding the obvious economic context, external legal spend continues to rise.

- **Managing demand** - Some teams identified an efficiency conundrum – the better we get, the busier we get. We at LBC Wise Counsel see this a great deal in many of our of consulting projects and it can force teams to retreat back to a more reactive role, as well as having a dampening effect on morale.

- **Relationships are still key** – However, it appears to be the case that in-house teams are most valued when the relationships with business colleagues are at their closest and most trusted, and that in these situations approachability and availability are valued highly. Teams consistently refer to trust and integrity as being significant indicators of value for them.

- **Reporting value is weak** - Few teams seem able to demonstrate efficiency improvement and to track their progress. We believe there is a lack of meaningful reporting that goes beyond identifying the volume of activity.

- **A lack of transparency and value in legal spending** - The cost and value of the service is not as transparent as it needs to be. We think too many teams do not have a clear enough view of what they spend, whom they spend it with and whether that spend represents value for money.

- **It is still not entirely clear what the role is** - The role of the legal team could be better defined. This is what we sometimes call the "elephant" syndrome; something which is quite hard to describe, but you definitely would know one when you see one! In other words in-house legal teams are very good at doing their job, less good at describing why it is valuable. We tend to the view that this, in turn, makes it harder for in-house teams to live up to the broader role that their unique position within their organisation gives them.

- **Legal remain a stable repository for know-how** - What is very noticeable is that there is often significant turnover of key staff in many business functions that rely on the in-house legal team, resulting in the legal team being the custodians of much historical and useful background knowledge (sometimes called "corporate memory").

The threats and blocked avenues

Our headline conclusion is that we consider that the general economic climate, combined with already stretched resource, presents a series of significant threats to the cohesiveness of in-house legal teams and their value to business.

The threats are more or less visible in a number of contexts, but are characterised in a number of ways:

- There is a sense of some teams (whether by accident or design) retreating from a pro-active role, the view being that such a role, while superficially attractive, does little except raise expectation, increase demand and stretch already thin resources.

- Some teams have adopted a near exclusive crisis management role, but this in turn has become a rather debilitating and morale sapping cycle – a bit like trying to empty water from a leaking boat but where the bucket is always smaller than the amount of water that is leaking in.

- It is clear, for example, that there is a genuine concern about the mismatch of resource and potential demand which is stifling a more strategic (and therefore possibly more valuable) role. We certainly detect that, if in-house resources are not aligned to business objectives, it is very easy for in-house teams to become overwhelmed with work.

- We see this as a potential weakness in the ability of some General Counsel to define and articulate a role that is more than operational and demand led. We also note that for many in-house teams the perception the business has of its General Counsel is the perception the business also has of the wider team – in other words the General Counsel becomes the personification of the team's strengths and its weaknesses.

- We remain concerned to see many legal teams still professing that to be valued by their non-lawyer colleagues they have to exceed expectations, fundamentally confusing relationship management with trying to please people. The aim, always, of such resource-stretched teams should be to define expectation and to meet it.

- Interestingly, we have also detected that email, far from being an aid to easier communication, has actually become a significant barrier to good communication. While it may be unfashionable to suggest that technology is not the answer to greater efficiency, we believe communication skills deteriorate the more reliant we become on the brusque, two-dimensional medium that is email. Our strong view is that legal teams (and law firms) have to make a conscious effort not to become over-reliant on email and to use the phone more, as well as to meet face-to-face.

- In addition, the search for meaningful Key Performance Indicators (KPIs) has become a rather half-hearted effort with teams resigned to believing that it is all too difficult; like the search for the Holy Grail there persists a belief that "out there", somewhere, some teams will have really great KPIs... so with little energy or enthusiasm, teams resort to a brief flirtation with two-dimensional measures that only tend to support the view that being busy is good enough.

- Finally, the perennial debate over managing low risk work persists. Virtually every team encounters the issue of having to deal with routine activity that silts-up the team and prevents then from either asserting a more pro-active role or undertaking more project based activity. In-house teams have to do more to manage the demand side of the equation and not simply look for solutions on the supply side.

What does this all amount to? It is clear, as it always has been, that in-house teams cope with prodigious workload and mostly tackle the requirements placed upon them with good humour and an abundance of professional integrity.

We conclude that value is not defined well enough and, therefore, not articulated well enough. As a consequence this may even mean that some in-house legal teams risk being seen as change resistant, inflexible and non-strategic.

We believe the debates showed that in-house teams add great value and have the potential to add even more, but we also believe there is a considerable risk that an opportunity will be missed if they do not effect some quite significant change.

The opportunity

The frustration we see is palpable in many teams - most teams can articulate the issues (as this report has just demonstrated!) but how do they solve the problems they know exist?

We believe there are some really insightful and interesting points to make from the debates. They identify the issues, but none of the points made presents either an easy or a necessarily straightforward way to proceed. Perhaps the first step on the journey is to accept that not everything can be done, or should be done, by an individual lawyer or in-house legal team however resourceful and committed they may be.

Perhaps we need to see in-house lawyers not as some sort of encyclopaedic repository of wisdom to be consulted like a mystical and sainted oracle, but as merely one type of "delivery system" for dispensing advice and guidance. As such they are but one of many systems for delivery of advice and the challenge/opportunity therefore is to develop others and to match the means of delivery with the real need of the business.

Other "delivery systems" would include, for example:

- Law firms

- Intranet/extranet

- Self-help tools
- Internal training
- Developing more automated processes

The point of this is not to make light of the lawyer's personal role, but to realise that it is a precious resource to be handled thoughtfully.

Should we, for example, employ people who take nearly seven years to fully qualify, and another two to four years to be creatively useful, and make them answer queries that could be looked up on the internet for free? If one can stop to consider this situation, it seems clear that far too much time is spent dealing with matters that could and should have a cheaper delivery system.

In essence we are saying that the in-house team has to take a step back from the operational maelstrom and not only define a role for itself which meets expectation, manages risk and looks at the wider role, but also recognises that it has to manage the demand side of the workflow equation and meet demand in more imaginative ways.

We therefore need to find ways to reuse know-how and to embed that know-how into the business. We also need to reallocate resources to where they will generate the most value and then we need to measure and acknowledge the impact all this has, so that we can demonstrate the value.

In doing so it will become easier (if not easy) to ensure that the legal team's objectives are aligned to those of the business and to better understand what the business considers valuable and important. But there is another genuinely fundamental point to make and that is that legal teams must also do more to manage the demand side of the legal services equation.

While we consider it crucial that in-house lawyers are creative around how they deploy resource, they must also be prepared to manage demand much more robustly. To take the point further regarding "systems of delivery", sometimes some work should simply not be done at all. This is about managing expectation as a core skill and was reiterated throughout the debate series. In summary, relationship management is not about pleasing people, but about doing the right things.

We do not advocate switching off service like a blown fuse; we do say there must be a dialogue with colleagues about what is done, when it is done and how it is done (or not) as the case may be.

Concluding thoughts – past success may not indicate future growth or even stability

If all this sounds a little cold, we are also certain that very significant value is derived from lawyers who are seen to be good team players, managers, leaders, coaches and mentors.

Legal teams that become truly value adding move away from the purely operational and assume a role that embraces a more strategic dimension; they find the time to consider unmet legal need, to analyse the risk environment and to develop the means to transfer know-how into the business.

Fundamentally this means establishing a different type of relationship with external law firms; not one based just on factors such as cost and legal expertise, but built around using the extended resource of a law firm and treating the available internal and external team as part of a single and seamless service.

Crucially there must also be the means to report value, to see trends and to make decisions based on data rather than gut feeling. This might be achieved with technology (although many proprietary software systems suffer from being originally designed for law firms rather than in-house teams), through benchmarking and through testing perceptions with those who use the service.

We are surprised and disappointed that more is not done to demonstrate value through measures and objectively derived data, but we do see this as a tremendous opportunity for teams to be able to develop something important and meaningful that works in their world. In a way this harks back to earlier comments about

KPIs and our conclusion here is that rather than seeking performance indicators derived from generic views of what value means, there should be a more personal and focussed effort to find the measures or metrics that matter to each organisation and to target improvement in these issues.

For law firms the challenge is not to trade on the short term profitability that is the inefficiency of the status quo, but to take a strategic investment in developing core relationships, enhancing these (perhaps at some real cost to the law firm) so that these rock solid relationships can demonstrate their value for the longer term, time and time again.

What is clear is that, while every team can make some reasonable attempt to describe value from its activity and the law firms they use can claim to be committed partners, the potential for a new type of relationship and for value to be derived in much more sophisticated ways is not yet part of the mainstream.

Our concern is that, if the threats we describe weaken the resolve to search for better ways to deliver value, the progress made by many in-house legal teams will stall. Now is the time to really push for something demonstrably valuable, not just for the lawyers, but for their employing business too.

Series two - The value of the in-house lawyer:

The following 12 points represent a distillation of the key points made in the debates. These points are not grouped or prioritised, but we think they make an interesting overview of the qualities and attributes of a great in-house lawyer. In later sections of this report we will examine the threat some of these points represent and also the great opportunity for in-house lawyers to make a lasting and significant impact on their businesses.

The 12 indicators of value:

1. **Leadership** – This idea, and what it stands for, covers such a wide spectrum of opinion that it probably

deserves a whole report to itself. It was consistently raised in the debates as an issue. In-house lawyers look to their General Counsel not just for management and mentoring support, but also to lead the team with the business. While most lawyers felt that they were reasonably well managed, far fewer felt that their General Counsel showed the qualities of leadership they wanted. We will return to this theme later in the report.

2. **Politically aware** – Most of the lawyers concluded that being politically aware was an essential skill; not to play politics themselves, but to better understand why things happen and how they happen in their organisations.

3. **Commercially aware** – It is an old chestnut, but was noted time and again. In many ways it is linked to being politically aware, but definitely is not about just giving the news that business colleagues want to hear.

Very often the word "commercial" is used negatively in feedback from business colleagues, so that, for example, "the legal team are not commercial enough", is really a euphemism for "not telling us what we want to hear"! Commerciality, done well, is about understanding the business and what drives its success.

Commercial awareness is a more complex idea than "taking a view" because it is expedient to do so; it is in fact much more closely aligned to personal credibility and being trusted than about notions of what is and is not commercial.

4. **Financially aware** — Many in-house lawyers commented on the need to be better equipped to understand some, at least, of the financial and economic drivers for their businesses. It is a common point of criticism made by business colleagues that lawyers do not have sufficient grasp of where and how companies make their money. This may be as simple as talking the language of the business,

but done well it plays very powerfully in terms of building personal credibility.

5. **Service orientated** – For most lawyers a strong service ethic is valued highly, particularly it seems as between lawyers. Seeing the job through, doing what it takes and stoic steadfastness are all elements of service that are valued by lawyers when they see these characteristics in other lawyers.

Interestingly, many business colleagues seem to value these qualities a little less. It might be unfair, but it might also be a salutary point as well that working late night after night is as likely to be seen as a sign of inefficiency as it is a sign of dedication.

6. **Flexibility** – This is a key skill. There is no doubt that in-house lawyers have to be able to juggle priorities, look at new issues and be able to look to the future in more immediate ways than would typically be the case for lawyers in law firms. A truism may be, but every day can be different and it is crucial not to be fazed by the twists and turns of an atypical day.

7. **Wants and seeks feedback** – At the heart of all miscommunication is "the assumption"; as soon as the phrase "but I assumed that…" is uttered, there is every chance something has gone wrong! Assumptions devalue advice because they short-cut relevancy and usefulness. For in-house lawyers this is tantamount to laziness and is totally avoidable.

Related to this point is the need to test how well we are doing. This is not about seeking personal endorsement, but about testing the relevancy of advice, ease of use, accessibility etc. so that we can ensure we are doing the right things in the right way.

8. **Risk sensitive** – A very significant quality for in-house lawyers is to be risk sensitive, but not risk averse. This skill is developed largely as a direct result of understanding the tolerance to risk within

the business and then tailoring guidance to be empathetic with the assessment made.

9. **Drives for improvement** – While it risks sounding clichéd, it is vital that in-house lawyers take responsibility for their own personal development and career progression. We believe that three-years' qualified lawyers today, perhaps in their late twenties and in their first in-house role, will change jobs on average every three to five years. We also believe that General Counsel will typically move every three years, matching the cycle of CEOs in many businesses.

10. **Communication expert** – No surprise that this should feature, but clearly crucial. In the end the role of any lawyer is to communicate well. We judge this to mean having an adaptive style that changes for the audience, with the scale of the threat and with the importance of the issues concerned. We also believe that lawyers have to show innovation in communication – it is a crowded air space and to be both heard and understood is becoming increasingly challenging.

11. **Consistency** – This is perhaps a sub-set of personal credibility, but the point is well made; to be perceived as apolitical, steadfast and dependable might not be the sexiest of characteristics, but they are very reassuring in the fast-paced and sometimes flawed world of business.

12. **Personal credibility** – Like "leadership" this is an intangible quality. In essence it is at the heart of being a great lawyer. To be trusted, to be asked to comment not because people have to take account of your views, but because they want to take account of your views, is really the pinnacle of acceptance and value. We judge this quality more highly than all the others as it captures the true value of the adviser.

These dozen characteristics represent the views of in-house lawyers as to the essential skills, behaviours and attributes of the in-house role. All are capable of development; none should be left to chance.

The qualities of an in-house lawyer – Threats, pitfalls and missed opportunities

In this section of the report, we put our interpretation on the feedback given in the series of debates on the value of the in-house lawyer.

Our headline conclusion is that individually and collectively in-house lawyers risk failing to assert their value in ways that business colleagues will recognise and in so doing will appear to be the caricature of a lawyer, grey, formal, samey and self-interested.

The threat, as we see it, is really exemplified in the list of 12 characteristics suggested in the debates representing the key qualities of a successful in-house lawyer. If legal expertise is taken as a given (in other words, if we do not challenge the absolute need for lawyers to know the law), the list of 12 characteristics represents a very powerful checklist for structuring and monitoring personal development at every stage of the lawyer's career.

However, in all the conversations we held with in-house lawyers, while the need for personal development was accepted and enthusiastically embraced, only a few were able to articulate how their personal journeys would be informed by the development of the 12 characteristics.

What can be done to raise the profile and importance of personal development? We think four points are crucially important:

- **You have got to make time for personal development.**

In recent studies we have conducted, the amount of time allocated for personal development is small and reducing. There are approximately 230 working days in the year; if just 5% of time was given to personal development, that would amount to about 12 days, or one day per month.

However, we typically see lawyers align personal development with the requirement to obtain Continuing Professional Development hours (CPD). This requirement averages at about two to three days a year, but in reality is often achieved by undertaking a series of free one or two-hour up-date workshops held by law firms and is about as far removed from insightful personal development as it is possible to get.

Our guidance is for lawyers to commit to a minimum of six days of personal development a year – less than 2.5% of the available time.

- **Plan personal development.**

If we treat our career as our most valuable asset - one generating income over perhaps 40 years to maintain both a lifestyle while in work and a pension out of work; one that creates a stimulating, emotionally and intellectually rewarding environment; and one that provides challenges by which we learn and grow as human beings, would we expect the development of skills essential to our success to be so half-heartedly considered?

It is a rhetorical question, but we must be self-critical; for most in-house lawyers, CPD is a chore, to be squeezed into a hectic life somehow. It hardly matters what we do as long as we get to the magical 16 hours!

Instead, of course, we should be examining our relative weakness against the 12 indicators of value and judging how we will find the thoughtful, well planned and important opportunities we need to improve.

- **It doesn't have to cost a lot (if anything), so don't use "lack of budget" as your excuse.**

It is of course possible, probably likely, that for some personal development some budget will be needed, but we consider that networking opportunities (local and national), some mentoring opportunities (which can be arranged within your business or between contacts made through networking) and learning in-depth about one's business, can all be achieved at no cost except for the personal commitment needed.

- **It is your career and it is your responsibility to make sure it develops, not your employer's responsibility.**

Obviously if you are lucky enough to work in an environment where personal development is at the heart of things, make sure you take advantage of this and use the opportunity to the full; but if you work in a more hard-pressed team where training is not such a priority, make sure you make it your responsibility to invest energy and time in your personal development.

The qualities of an in-house lawyer - A different perspective, valued, thoughtful and innovative

So, our debates have revealed 12 characteristics of being a great in-house lawyer. The list is not an exclusive set of competencies and no doubt other obvious competencies can be articulated as well, but it is, even so, a fascinating insight. What does this say about the role of an in-house lawyer?

As we explored in the first report, there are many roles for in-house teams, some are very operationally orientated, others more strategic, most exist somewhere between the two. The role of the in-house lawyer, however, is, we think, capable of being described more generically, notwithstanding the diverse role of teams or subject specialism.

We think the role can be described by reference to six key characteristics:

- **Leadership is for every lawyer**

"Leader" is a loaded word...it comes with the resonance of tub-thumping oratory, of "command and control", of self-awareness and it is not for everyone. However, in the context of the in-house lawyer, we think everyone has a leadership responsibility.

In our view, every lawyer needs to be able to lead opinions, to influence, persuade and cajole; every lawyer has to want to occasionally stand aside from the crowd, to put his or her head above the parapet, to hold out for what is right, not always what is expedient.

• Provide a different perspective

We are drawn to sculpture and to art generally very often because it provides a different perspective. It challenges us to consider our world in a different way, to value more what we might once have valued less.

We don't make the clumsy point that lawyers are now somehow artists, but we do make the point that it is the lawyer's job to describe the business world in the context of legal risk, to shine a light on a different perspective and to make our non-lawyer colleagues value something more that they might once have valued less.

• Innovate

In-house teams will never be resourced to meet all the demand a business will have for legal advice. In-house lawyers will always grapple with competing priorities and will always have to solve the perennial conundrum that is the balance between being reactive and proactive.

The only solution is to be innovative - innovative in the way demand is managed, law firms used, information provided, training delivered, technology used.

In the end it will be the duty of all lawyers to look at their role and be creative around how they deliver a service to their business so that demand is managed as effectively as possible.

• Be aware

Time and again our research tells us that the more lawyers understand their businesses, the more effective their guidance becomes. Non-lawyer colleagues are naturally drawn to those lawyers who are enthusiastic for their world, their products and their processes. Finance people respect lawyers who can read the balance sheet and who can deliver guidance sensitive to the P&L implications.

This isn't rocket science, but it is at the heart of the role. In the 12 characteristics identified, three were about awareness – be politically aware, financially aware, commercially aware – probably best summarised as simply being aware.

- Be valued

To be valued, lawyers have got to do more than be able to do valuable things; lawyers have to be able to articulate value as well. The ability to communicate well, to be understood and to have guidance followed is obviously a key skill.

Communication is quicker and easier in our virtual world, but being an effective communicator is probably much harder. Real thoughtfulness is now required and there is much to learn.

- Build personal credibility

"Trust me I am a lawyer" risks being considered an oxymoron.

No one should trust you just because you are a lawyer; they should trust you because you have a track record of resolute trustworthiness, of consistent, timely and valued delivery, of unwavering professionalism, of empathic creativity, of being approachable to all, but nobody's fool.

"Trust me because I have shown you can trust me…" is the space to occupy.

It is hard even for lawyers to judge which of a group of lawyers is the best technical lawyer, but it is easy for anyone to form a judgement on whom they would like to work with and who they feel will do the best job. This is not a fatuous judgment; in the end personal credibility is probably 80% of the role.

Concluding thoughts - It is within our own hands, no permissions needed

This report has considered the question of what value means in terms of the individual in-house lawyer. The debates on value elicited 12 characteristics and we have distilled these to the six we consider to be the most important. Describing how in-house lawyers should set about a personal development programme that would enhance these six (or even all 12) competencies is not easy in its detail, but the following more general points will apply to most of us:

1. Make your personal development a priority and plan for it. Why not, in fact, create a business plan for your career, not just for a year, but for three years or longer?

2, Be prepared to network. Dale Carnegie said: "You can make more friends in two months by becoming interested in other people than you can in two years trying to get other people to be interested in you…" Your network will sustain you in many ways and it is never too late to start.

3. Have a mentor; a trusted colleague, someone from your network, a colleague in the business – someone whose opinion you value and who will invest a little time in you.

4. Treat personal development seriously. CPD is not an audit tick box requirement. Take the time to work out what is best for you, research programmes and seek out opinions.

5. Find a soft skills programme you value. Keeping up to date with the law is relatively easy, but finding where you can develop some at least of the 12 characteristics of a great in-house lawyer will not be so straightforward.

6. Don't wait for permission to develop your skills; the lights are already on green and for 80% of this you do not need a budget, just the personal drive to take on the challenge.

The role of the in-house lawyer is changing and will change more radically still as new business models are developed to meet the challenge of the Legal Services Act; this series of debates has illuminated many significant points is, and we think, a valuable contribution to defining the value of an in-house lawyer.

Series three – The value of the relationship with law firms:

The following ten points represent a distillation of the most consistent themes that were discussed in the debates. These points are not grouped or prioritised, but we think they make an interesting overview of the qualities and attributes that characterise great relationships and therefore of the issues that help to add significant value.

The ten indicators of value:

1. **Service first**—There is really no getting away from the fact that first and foremost relationships succeed when law firms provide a great service. Fundamentally this is about ensuring the client interests are understood and then met, but it is also about the sensitive deployment of resource and expertise.

   Law firms have to show that they can get deals done, win cases, settle disputes and advise with skill and some flare; but in doing so they must also act without arrogance, show empathy and thoughtfulness and, crucially, maintain proportionality in the scope and cost of their activity.

   The essence of this indicator is "trust" and while the core skill of the lawyer (to know the law) is at the heart of this concept, it is only truly valued when associated with significant relationship development skills as well.

2. **Teamwork** – This sense of relationship development is in part, at least, about moving beyond the instructed activity to a place where the contributions of in-house legal team and law firm can be seen to enhance the experience and to improve the probability of successful outcomes.

   Both law firm and in-house team have key roles to play in establishing the teamwork ethos, but it is incumbent on the law firm to be open to some discretionary activity which invests in the relationship and which does not incur additional costs for the client. While firms should not be treated as if they are charitable foundations and expected to give up vast swathes of time for free, there is a mutual advantage to establishing the depth and breadth of the relationship and a significant amount of time should be given freely to achieve this.

3. **Value v Cost** — Many in-house teams feel a little vulnerable when instructing outside lawyers; this vulnerability is often a factor of concern expressed by colleagues who do not necessarily understand the advantage and necessity of using a law firm when, as they see it, there is a perfectly adequate lawyer working in-house.

One of the ways this concern can be allayed is for the law firm to constantly seek out opportunities to articulate value and to bolster the image of the in-house team. This is not to be done in any self-serving way, but requires law firms to appreciate that to many in the client organisation they will be perceived as an extremely expensive overhead. If they are also perceived to be expensive and unnecessary, it is hard for all concerned to build their credibility. Law firms must therefore be alive to all possibilities for helping clients and in-house teams to realise the full value of the engagement; in effect not just on the matter in hand, but in the lessons to be learned, in process improvement, in knowledge transfer etc..

4. **It starts on day one** — This is a salutary point for many law firms. The day a relationship begins is the first day in the effort to successfully re-tender for that work. As we know, it is increasingly the case that law firms are appointed to act for clients based on some formal tendering process. This might result in a panel, or a preferred supplier list, but even when that is not the case, it is still nevertheless indicative of decisions

to appoint that are based on some sort of transparent evaluation criteria.

Re-tendering in two or three years time should be less risky if in the meantime every opportunity is taken by law firms to engage with the client and to seek feedback as well as articulate value. That's why it starts on day one.

5. **Think not just about the legal issues, but about how the client works** – This point clearly builds on earlier remarks, but must not be underestimated.

The difference between advice which is technically correct and advice which adds value is very often a question of context and accessibility. Fundamentally most firms can deliver technically correct advice; true value therefore is realised only when the client/in-house team can quickly and easily assimilate the guidance and use it to their advantage.

The law firms that continually take the trouble to understand how the client works (policy, process, people, politics etc.) can also increase the likelihood that their advice will be well received and useful.

6. **Flexibility and feedback** – For law firms these are both highly significant characteristics of a successful relationship.

Feedback is rarely sought in a systematic and consistent way. It is sometimes characterised by partners having an informal chat over lunch or at the rugby match, but needs to be elevated to a far more significant degree. Every aspect of the relationship should be under scrutiny and the client's strengths and weaknesses should be examined fully as well; in essence, there should be a commitment to find continuous improvement.

Flexibility is harder to describe as an abstract concept, but does require law firms to be able to act on feedback (and sometimes on their own intuition), for example, on the make-up of their team, on charging methodology, on risk-sharing and on many other things too. Crucially it is about putting the success of the relationship with the firm above the self-interest of individuals within the firm.

7. **Value-add conundrums** – For some clients the "value-add" is the list of additional services law firms will offer for free (training, secondments, legal updates etc.) that helps to bulk out the relationship; for others it is about embedding relationships within the client culture.

At its worst, it is a wish list with boxes ticked on day one that are seldom used afterwards. At its best, value-add can secure and deepen relationships, become part of the risk management process and develop and enhance the standing of the in-house team.

The challenge for law firms is not to be deflected by clients who appear less interested in value-add, but to maintain across the firm a belief in the benefit that can come from a significant and thoughtful investment in activities away from the legal advice. We believe that some firms are very sceptical about value-add; we think they often pay lip service to it anticipating that clients will be distracted from using it. However, as a point of differentiation at retendering, the successful delivery of a thoughtful and well designed programme of value-add is extremely powerful and not to be underestimated.

8. **Networking** – This might not appear to be an obvious element of a significant relationship, but the point was developed by many participants in the debates. The typical in-house team is very busy, perceives itself to be slightly under-resourced and lacks peer group support. On this basis, given the connections they can make, law firms are well placed to facilitate networking opportunities for their clients.

Law firms that create opportunities for in-house teams to network not only provide a social setting for informal connections to be made, but help create an environment for sharing ideas, exchanging know-how and accelerating best practices. Fundamentally networking is an underused, but essential skill and law firms are remarkably well placed to help their clients in this endeavour. Law firms that are committed to providing such opportunities informally underline their value and again create significant points of differentiation in a highly competitive environment.

9. **Drive for improvement** – The restless pursuit of continuous improvement is a significant quality that is highly valued by clients. The best relationships are characterised by self-critical analysis and a determination to cut out waste and deliver more value.

Law firms face an uphill battle in this regard when very often (still) their preferred charging model is based on hourly rates, but any long term relationship should result in process improvement, efficiency savings and service enhancement. The challenge is not to rely on this occurring by some form of professional osmosis, but through a determined drive for change and an analysis of systematically collected data and management information.

10. **Communication expert** – Finally, great relationships are characterised by the quality of the communication. It is an old chestnut, but the fact it is a clich does not diminish its significance. It is rarely perfect in any relationship, but there are elements of the communication process that can be worked on and improved. What is the preferred style, what are the preferred channels, how can tone be developed to add value, how can presentation be enhanced? – and so on.

It is not rocket science, but like the previous point it needs a focus and a specific level of engagement to ensure issues are addressed and opportunities identified. These ten characteristics represent the views of in-house lawyers as to the essential skills, behaviours and attributes of significant and valuable law firm relationships. There are probably no surprises in the list, but equally it is interesting to understand that, in the context of the debates, few firms were thought to deliver consistently high levels of performance against all these criteria.

The relationship with law firms - What next?

In this section of the report, we put our interpretation on the feedback given in the series of debates on the value of the relationship with law firms.

There will be much talk in the legal press in the months to come about how law firms need to shape up in the context of an economy in recession and to the challenge of deregulation. Commentators will propound new thinking, law firms may seek their insights, but the essence of great relationships is encapsulated in the feedback captured in this report from in-house teams up and down the country. Nothing fancy, nothing extraordinary, but basic steps consistently well executed.

We think that these fundamentals of relationship development have to be at the heart of any law firm strategy and they can be characterised as follows:

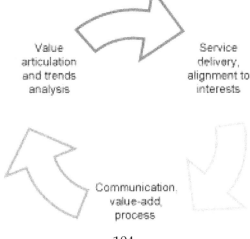

Value articulation and trends analysis

Service delivery, alignment to interests

Communication, value-add, process

104

This virtuous circle emphasises the need to drive for continuous improvement while focusing on how alignment to client interests, communication and value articulation enhance the core legal skills and provide points of differentiation.

This analysis also highlights how developing good existing relationships will be the foundation for future growth and success. In an environment where an increasing number of relationships are scrutinised routinely within procurement-style appointment (and reappointment) processes, law firms must see the investment in relationships as a strategic and operational imperative.

The quality and value of relationships, of course, is dependent on the level of commitment of both parties and so law firms can only really improve to the extent that in-house teams are committed to improvement.

The challenge for law firms is to push against an ineffectual client to ensure they manage the risk of failing to adequately differentiate their proposition. The challenge for in-house teams is to make sure that their colleagues see the value and quality of the service provided by law firms and that they exploit the value-add opportunity for themselves.

Concluding thoughts

The tried and trusted three letter acronym used to be CRM — Client Relationship Management; - but in our view it is a limiting concept that has its place in a rather defensive and uninspiring mindset.

We believe the future, albeit driven by cost saving and efficiency improvement in this harsh economic environment, is better described by the acronym CRD — Client Relationship Development - where both law firm and in-house team creatively engage to maximise the contribution each can make seeking ever closer alignment to interests, a commitment to innovation, process improvement and value articulation.

In summary, success is not about relationships that are predicated on a temporary convergence of interests, but on embedded, shared values and a commitment to common goals with long- term ambition.

20. Is now a good time to become a lawyer?

To read some lawyers' contributions to the legal blogs you might be forgiven for thinking that becoming a lawyer today was not the shrewdest career choice one could make. It is certainly true to say that some firms are cancelling (or postponing) training contracts, that the legal profession (in the UK at least) is soul searching whether the partnership model is dead and I suspect we all think that the time of super rich (if never easy) pickings for the stars of the profession may also appear to be disappearing fast.

In short, given this context, if you are about to embark on a career as a lawyer you might find it much, much harder to get started; then, once you are started, the traditional career model is in a state of flux and even if you get to be very good at what you do, you might not earn as much as partners in law firms have been used to earning in years gone by.

Okay then – it is time for a serious reality check and for you to answer the one big question: Why do you want to be a lawyer?

If you want to be a lawyer because:

- You will sit in a big swivelling leather chair, behind an imposing desk on one of the upper floors of an award winning swanky steel and glass cathedral to the great god of the corporate big-shot; or

- You want to earn enough money to have disposable income even after you have paid alimony to at least two divorced spouses; or

- You think you look good in bespoke chalk-stripe suits; or

- You relish the idea of working on deals at 3am and shouting at trainees (because you used to be shouted at and it didn't do you any harm); or

- You want to have a photograph on your imposing desk of the second home in the country that you never have time to visit

...then I guess you really should now pause for thought, because on this basis it is my analysis that your career choice may not turn out as you want. I suspect (in fact, I hope) that the world is quickly moving away from such perceptions.

But what if you want to be a lawyer for different reasons? And what if those reasons might be even more important now than ever before? Four reasons like these:

1. What if, for example, you have a passion for the Rule of Law?

Are you someone who sees the law not just as a tool for developing extraordinarily complex tax arrangements and financial instruments, but as a means to ensure that competitive advantage for business is achieved by doing the right things well?

Do you see the law not just as a means to exert economic power, but as a means to hold the powerful to account and to ensure that regulatory systems protect those who need protection while not stifling innovation and entrepreneurialism? Do you see the law not as a fig leaf for excess and laissez-faire, but front and centre in a more ethically orientated world?

2. What if you have a passion for a profession based on its own highly developed ethical code?

Lawyers as officers of the court answerable for their conduct, so that how lawyers work is just as important as what they work on; lawyers as dedicated men and women who have to put their clients' interests ahead of their own, always acting in the best interests of those they represent - Isn't that the most extraordinary obligation in this day and age, but isn't it also an obligation that will help to build trust in a world where trust has been a tradable commodity in so many areas of our lives?

3. What if you have a sense of personal vocation?

Are you passionate about making a difference, for example for the poor and oppressed in your community, or in a political environment where you want to help develop laws locally and nationally that make your society fairer? Or perhaps you are passionate about helping a business you believe in - one that you want to help make a success for its employees, customers and shareholders.

4. What if the old professional structures in any event are not for you?

There is a very good argument to suggest that the traditional business model for law firms actually makes it harder for women to succeed, or for minorities to progress and that it doesn't offer anything much for those who do not aspire to climb the greasy pole to partnership. Perhaps for you the new business structures that could embrace diversity, entrepreneurialism and offer creative flexible career paths might be a very attractive alternative. Perhaps, indeed, you might help shape and run such businesses.

Personally speaking, and I know it is tough right now, I don't think there has been a more important time to be a lawyer or a more important time to assert the values that ensure the profession adapts to the renewed expectations of our society - expectations of trust, probity, integrity, thoughtfulness and care.

These are undoubtedly difficult times, but I am certain that more than ever we need our lawyers to be at the top of their game and I am sure as well that there has never been a more important time for young lawyers to come forward and excel.

21. Tell me something I can take away and do...

Speaking with one General Counsel the other day, I was asked a not untypical question: "What can you tell me that I could implement today that will help me and my team become more effective?" I guess we all hope there might be something we can do better that is relatively easy and inexpensive to fix, but too often we spend our time searching for complex, clever and often expensive solutions.

So let's get back to some basics; here are my top ten things that you could implement today:

1. Get a mentor. Find someone inside or outside of your business, someone whose judgement you trust to be your sounding board and guide. I have had the same mentor for nearly twenty years; in fact I now know him so well, I sometimes don't even have to speak with him because I can just imagine what he would say! General Counsel is a lonely role, without a great deal of peer support and it is not always easy to network. It makes great sense therefore to have someone you trust to discuss your plans, hopes, fears and ambitions. It is possibly the most important appointment to your team you will ever make.

2. You will almost always feel under-resourced; when I discuss headcount with senior lawyers they invariably tell me, "If I had just one more lawyer..." The way to fix this is not to recruit, but to decide what you can realistically deliver to your business with one fewer lawyer; manage activity to that headcount and, lo and behold, you will have your extra lawyer. This is not as daft an idea as it may sound because in any event by the time you account for holiday and

sickness leave you already have less resource than your spreadsheets and budgets tell you.

3. Prioritise not just by urgency, but by where in your business the issues arise; in other words focus the majority of your time and energy where your business makes the most money, carries the most risk or where reputational harm can be inflicted. This is unsophisticated alignment, but it is crucial for your credibility. As one CEO once explained to me, "Put your lawyers where the profit is, not where there is most noise."

4. Articulate value all the time - not just in WIP reports, but in all your informal and formal interaction with colleagues. "Why should any business employ you?" is a question you should live with every day; is it because you are cheaper, more accessible, more knowledgeable; because you pre-empt, avoid, mitigate, train, inform, deliver? Whatever it is, make sure it is known and understood.

5. Focus more on delivering great service and less on content. Clearly content has to be accurate and relevant; but is it also timely, accessible, understandable, uncomplicated, directional, unambiguous, thoughtful and given to the right people, in the right way at the right time? I am in no doubt personally that delivery is more important than content.

6. Train for soft skills in a systematic, thoughtful and planned way. Typically in-house teams spend 80% of their training budget on legal update training, but surely we know enough law (or we can at least find out what the law is)? Someone said to me once that we know the most law the day after our last finals exam; from that day onward we lose our knowledge of laws and replace it with experience. Our soft skills (influencing, presentation, communication, negotiation etc.) are the means by which we convey our expertise and judgement; without them we are

almost impotent as advisers. So make sure you train these skills and rely less on a sort of professional osmosis for your team's improvement.

7. Be conversant, at least, with your own business's profit and loss accounts and balance sheets. You will never be credible in your business if you are not able to interpret how your business makes money, invests in its future, manages cost, cashflow and distributes income. You don't have to be an accountant, but you do have to be comfortable with and interested in the financial framework that underpins your world.

8. Go to lunch at different times! How trite is that?! But it is astonishing how we get into routines; we lunch at the same time, sit at the same table, with the same colleagues etc. Our work is predicated on know-how and much of that know-how is only useful when our informal networks are as good as they can be. So called "water-cooler" conversations are vital and the more people we are connected to the better we deliver our service. Going to lunch at different times may not be a panacea to networking, but at least make sure you give some thought to how you can be better connected within your business.

9. Use email less and voicemail more. We all say the same things about email -"Couldn't do without it…" etc. etc., but equally we complain that it doesn't carry nuance, is too easy, too blunt, too quick. We treat it almost as if it were an informal conversation, when often it becomes a document of record. Voicemail however carries a level of nuance, literally tone of voice, a sense of priority and genuine urgency as well as empathy and thoughtfulness. Something I often ask new recruits is not to answer any internal email by email, but in the first two weeks or so to ring or call on colleagues; it is the quickest and best way to accelerate their introduction into the business.

10. Finally, say "No" sometimes. You are not a full service team, you never were and you never will be. And you

will not be thought less of either. Many non-lawyer colleagues mistake your willingness to do anything as a sign of your underutilisation! In any event relationships are established in business by doing the right things at the right time; be admired for your efficiency not for being pathologically compliant. The frenetic pace, long hours and crisis management that characterise many in-house teams are features that are not generally admired; they are instead thought to be rather bewildering and if the team was much bigger (not a funny little enclave of legaldom), it would come under much closer management scrutiny.

So, there you are, ten points with no implementation cost, no cap-ex, no op-ex…no-brainer.

22. Preparing to succeed

Frankly, for any business and therefore for any law firm, the worldwide recession is so enormous in its scope and impact, so all encompassing and so dependent on political intervention that it is impossible to set out a step-by-step guide to preparing for the recovery.

That said, I believe there are things that law firms could and should be doing now to prepare for the recovery and in this article I explore these ideas in more detail. In addition, when the recovery comes, it will be accompanied by a new regulatory framework for legal services and this must also be a significant factor when preparing to succeed. I believe five factors will help determine the success or otherwise of law firm strategy:

1. Alignment with profitable activity and profitable clients

2. Differentiation from competitors

3. Innovation in service delivery and pricing

4. Lawyers skilled to be business consultants, not just competent lawyers

5. Leveraging know-how, not associates

1. Alignment with profitable activity and profitable clients

It is often said to us by senior partners, somewhat sheepishly, that 80% of a law firm's profit is derived from 20% of its clients. This may just be a coincidence of the firms we are talking to, but it strikes me that, if this is anything like a normal distribution pre-recession, then, post-recession, law firms will have to think very differently.

As this present market tightens its grip on all businesses forcing cuts in every budget, it is impossible to imagine that clients will spend money on lawyers in the future in the same way ever again. Transparency and control are going to be watchwords for the long term.

The 20% of clients that helped to provide such a substantial living for lawyers in years gone by are almost bound to show less largesse and the 80% of clients who were allowed to hang around because they presumably provided a triumph of hope over experience will have to diminish significantly – for law firms, their presence will become literally unaffordable.

The challenge for law firms at this time, therefore, is to migrate their activity from managing an unsustainably broad base including a great many essentially unprofitable clients and to focus, instead, on broadening the base of profitable clients. In doing so the number of clients a firm chooses to act for will almost certainly reduce and the management time and energy that is applied to looking after passive and less valuable clients will be directed, instead, to managing active, significant clients and contacts.

2. Differentiation from competitors

In a world where everyone is blind, as the saying goes, the one eyed man is king.

In a world where law firms have until now barely had to scratch the surface of what makes them stand out in the market and special to their clients, there is going to be marketing revolution. Those businesses that can establish clear points of differentiation from their competitors in terms of brand, service perception, niche market expertise, delivery channels, pricing etc. will have a key strategic advantage.

The questions that must now be asked include:

- What is the firm's ideal client profile in terms of sector and turnover?

- What do clients say about your firm and what do you want them to say?

- What do prospective clients think about your firm and what do you want them to think?

In fact, in summary, are you ready to make an in-depth and strategically significant investment in obtaining and analysing feedback and then in building your brand values?

3. Innovation in service delivery and pricing

The end of hourly billing is a recurring theme, because it now so clearly has momentum; in my judgement any pricing model that is based on the six minute unit of charge and hourly rates is not a long term pricing structure the profession can rely on.

Put bluntly, clients in a recession want their lawyers to be able predict two things, cost and outcomes. This mindset is very unlikely to change when the recession comes to an end and so law firms will have to get used to finding the means both to share more risk and to fix/cap their prices.

In addition clients increasingly want legal guidance provided to them in a variety of more accessible ways, for example, based on templates, or through an ongoing investment in their own intranets, hotlines for their HR teams and diagnostic tools for their in-house legal department.

By implication clients also want less face time with expensive partners; instead there is a growing acceptance of the practice of establishing more points of contact within the client team with less senior colleagues and non-lawyer colleagues.

All this means that clients are moving away from demanding consultative time in meetings and instead they are seeking more instantly available and/or easily transferable know-how.

4. Lawyers skilled to be business consultants, not just competent lawyers

Consultative time becomes the premium end service, to be used strategically and for maximum impact; so, when clients demand consultative time with their lawyers, they will not want disconnected scholarly legal advice that appears to have been mystically derived from the cloistered vacuum of an independent mind. What they will want is practical, insightful wisdom, expressed plainly and concisely, clothed in the client's vocabulary, delivered to the people who need it most and in a form that needs no energy to apply it.

To give such advice requires skills that go far beyond a great academic law degree and far beyond a traditional training contract with a **galacticos** law firm.

Perhaps going forward the best lawyers will be equipped to be business consultants, not just good lawyers. Perhaps therefore we will need to ensure that they routinely have had the experience of a post-graduate MBA, a compulsory six month "seat" as part of their training contract on secondment in a major client, and, as they become more experienced, they will have enjoyed a period on secondment in a non-legal role to broaden their experience even more.

5. Leveraging know-how, not associates

This point picks up again on the know-how transfer message. It also alludes to the fact that the old model of treating associate lawyers a little like pit ponies (tethered underground for years of their career until they are perceived to be ready to see the daylight once more and work with humankind again) may not prove to be the most enlightened strategy on the planet.

Law firms going forward will need to proclaim not just that they have great people, but that they have great know-how too - the point being that leveraging know-how by packaging the firm's expertise in different ways will mean that it is used many times with different price points, different functionality and different risk/reward indices.

A firm that can take one piece of know-how and then develop many ways to use it will be a firm that can succeed in the new world order. It will indicate a cleverness in the way they value their "product" and will demonstrate a willingness to meet client expectations of innovation around service and the value of different types of services.

For example, one piece of know-how could be used in the following ways:

- Consulting with clients
- Training clients
- Training the trainers in clients
- Published to client desk-tops
- Published to know-how tools used within the client
- Through "blackberries" and cell-phones
- "White labelled" for the client to pass on to its clients (a sort of derivative in legal know-how!)

And each delivery channel, each type of know-how transfer, will have its own price point; each will also have its own enhanced service level and its basic service level and each delivery channel can be managed to share in a risk/reward strategy that provides the opportunity to make anything affordable to anyone.

The challenge for law firms is to be able to see when the current recessionary trough might be ending and then to be able to ride the recovery curve sufficiently well enough.

In doing so law firms must resist the temptation to replicate the old practices (however successful they might once have been), but must look instead to invest in a future world that is going to be characterised by two things:

- Clients who are much more empowered, who are seeking control, transparency and value.
- Regulatory regime that is facilitating wider and greater competition from within the profession and from outside.

These are tough times, but these are also times in which to regroup and to ensure that we all think strategically about our businesses. In this environment no one firm will have all the right answers, but we can all make sure we ask the right questions.

23. Supporting the support teams

Even in the best times some support functions in many law firms suffer from a downplaying of their value by their lawyer colleagues simply because their teams are not populated with lawyers doing 1400 (plus) chargeable hours a year.

However, in the current environment this attitude may prove to be even less enlightened than it always has been. There are three significant reasons to suggest that investing in (excellent) support functions helps to retain existing clients and secure new business. This is certainly true in good times and I suspect it will be even more important in these much more trying times. Support functions add value by:

Encouraging multiple points of contact with clients

Helping secure the value-add proposition

Assisting with the account management aspects of the relationship

These three activities are crucial to ensuring that clients see the value of the relationship.

1. Multiple points of contact

Developing multiple points of contact with any client helps to secure the relationship; it is like tethering a tent, the more tent pegs that are used the less likely the tent will succumb to any stormy weather. Equally, in the context of the law firm – in terms of client relationship management or development - the more points of contact there are, the more opportunity there is to see how value can be delivered.

Very often lawyers in law firms understand this principle only in the context of cross-selling to their lawyer colleagues, but in reality it is often easier and more cost-effective to sell in one's non-lawyer colleagues.

Consider, for example, how the librarian can support and in-house team; how the IT team might help build or develop the intranet capability of the in-house team; how the support lawyer cohort might help develop training materials for the in-house team to deliver to their business colleagues – and so on.

All are examples of relatively inexpensive points of contact, but each activity demonstrates commitment and delivers value. It also makes it harder to move away from the law firm on review; the thinking being that it makes little sense for a client to change its law firm when there are so many "mini" relationships that are established and which are delivering value.

Pull the support team back from the client and the law firm is left with only its lawyers to impress the client, with narrower lines of contact and looking more vulnerable to change.

2. Securing the value-add proposition

In the client's estimation, value-add can be a crucial part of the law firm proposition and for the law firm it is one of the better opportunities to demonstrate both commitment and value to the client.

The in-house team will most likely have a cumbersome bureaucracy to comply with within its business to gain the budget and the approval for any additional staff, for non-standard training, for their own IT solutions etc.; this is not always a question of expense; often it is just a tiresome process and so is not pursued.

If the in-house team can secure through the law firm some elements of training, additional resource through secondments and much more meaningful management information, it will improve its effectiveness significantly. Furthermore it is unlikely to cost the law firm a great deal in cash terms, but fixes them limpet-like to the client.

As this is not traditional territory for relationship partners and unlikely to be of great interest to them either, it is the support teams that can lift much of this burden off the desks of their lawyer colleagues in the firm. It can then become an accessible, lower cost and more administrative role that embeds relationships and supports the value proposition.

Pull the support team back from the client and the law firm is left with only its lawyers to impress the client, with narrower lines of contact and looking more vulnerable to change.

3. Account management

Not too many law firms operate account managers - in other words, colleagues who are not lawyers necessarily, but people assigned to a client to be its key contact for both accessing the right lawyers within the firm and supporting/coordinating the value-add proposition.

It is probably only relevant in the larger, multi-jurisdictional law firms, but having a "go-to" contact in the firm who can be called on as often as needed to help facilitate the whole relationship in the round, can be enormously helpful.

However accessible the lawyers are in any firm, the labyrinthine nature of many practices needs "de-coding"; making the firm accessible is therefore a vital role. The reassurance it provides helps to embed the relationship and, if it is done well, makes considering changing law firms almost unthinkable.

Pull the support team back from the client and the law firm is left with only its lawyers to impress the client, with narrower lines of contact and looking more vulnerable to change.

In my judgement, therefore, support teams are definitely not a luxury that should be considered dispensable, even in the current climate, without a great deal of thought. They are potentially a key differentiator for the law firm and, especially in these very difficult times, they represent a highly cost-effective client retention model.

The reality is that the more non-advisory activity is delegated to the support teams, the better the service is likely to be. Let's hear it for the backroom!

24. Not everything is an opportunity... but doing nothing is not an option

It will sound trite to say that in adversity there is always opportunity, especially when what we are collectively experiencing is probably the most significant recession since the Second World War, possibly ever, in the developed industrial world.

The now familiar daily commentary on the collapse of banks and the banking system around the world, has given everyone a new vocabulary; words such as "crunch" and "trillion" have entered our everyday conversation, but becoming used to the language does not make us any more likely to cope with the upheaval and change that is now thrust upon us all. No one can be in any doubt that this is fundamentally serious and potentially devastating and knowing the words will not be much help if the right decisions are not made about our businesses and the right actions do not immediately follow.

It is also clear now that one of the unintended and unforeseen consequences of the globalisation of commercial enterprise is that the complex interconnectivity of businesses, governments and systems (such as creditor insurance, supply chain, logistics etc.) can mean that one company's failure in one country can have disastrous consequences for thousands of businesses in many other countries.

In such times as these the direct negative impact on the legal profession may not be as harsh as in some sectors where supply chains are longer, margins thinner and where credit is in effect the blood-supply that oxygenates the vital organs of those industries. Rightly there will be no government rescues for law practices, but the impact of the recession on lawyers is still very real and will be long-lasting and significant.

So in a way it probably is certainly trite to talk of "opportunity" and it is obviously crucial to avoid sounding glib or superficial – real people are making real sacrifice and experiencing real uncertainty and discomfort – but, if we believe that there is no opportunity, the alternative mindset is to accept that we are all doomed to live forever with the negative consequences of macro-economic systemic and strategic failure - and that surely cannot be right either?

In this environment the legal profession and the legal services industry generally has no alternative but to take significant and far reaching steps, not only to manage the harsh economic realities of today (in terms of business structures, products and services), but also to drive for innovation, to be entrepreneurial and, I think crucially, to define and work with a new emphasis on business ethics as well.

Lawyers changing the way they work in order to be able to cut costs, changing to adapt to new markets and changing to meet a new client expectation has an obvious resonance now, but the consequences of a new era of compliance and supervision and of ethical trading has yet to be fully explored. But I believe that it will be front and centre in government policy, in the new remit of regulators everywhere and inevitably therefore in the boardroom as well…and lawyers, therefore, will have a major role to fulfil.

No longer will there be room just for the testosterone-fuelled, single-minded pursuit of the "can-do", "make it happen" attitude, but perhaps a space as well for a more reflective "should we do this", "should we do it this way" approach based on broad based professional integrity and on ensuring lawyers act in their clients' wider best interests.

In addition, and fundamentally, the profession in the UK must also address a second and potentially even more significant horizon, that of the Legal Services Act 2007 and the implications of a new competitive age.

Some will say that the Legal Services Act brings about unwelcome change, a dilution of professionalism and new entrants of doubtful credibility working to dubious standards where the pursuit of profit is a stronger driver than doing the right thing. Others will say that the legal profession helped to prop up our credit riddled economies, did nothing to act as a check or balance on boardroom excess and actually participated in that excess rather too vaingloriously for everyone else's good.

In reality, of course, while it is always convenient for commentators to polarise debate, the Legal Services Act is neither a Trojan horse full of malcontents and chancers nor a panacea for the consumer; but it is most certainly a reality. And, because it is a reality, the profession must work with it, develop it and make the best of it. In doing so, there is more to achieve than to lose, and in not doing so, the converse is true. These are therefore very significant times indeed, perhaps times the like of which we have not seen before and, as a result, it is incumbent on us all to consider our response and to act.

For those unfamiliar with the implications of the Legal Services Act or who are not immediately affected by it (not in practice in the UK perhaps), do not be fooled into a false sense of security. When the genie is out of this particular bottle, it will never go back in.

I don't think there is a King Canute option, because while some governments may seek to regulate to protect legal services delivered by fully qualified lawyers, spend just a few minutes trying to define what a legal service is and you will quickly realise that vast swathes of activity undertaken by lawyers is simply administrative and commercial. Change is coming - be in no doubt.

Hope, in this environment, is not a strategy.

So if to do nothing is to risk everything, the challenge for us all is to be able to examine and understand what is going on today, then to frame our responses in the light of what we can learn from others and to see the activity that we then engage in as an important part of our ability to manage our businesses and our careers in this downturn.

25. The value of all your people

In most businesses the people employed are the most expensive resource; this is even more so in the world of professional services where much of the product is delivered by people and where very often the product is the people. One of the most crucial debates, therefore, for any law firm at this time is how to retain and develop their best lawyers and staff while also making those prudent adjustments to overall headcount to ensure that the cost base is in step with predictable and sustainable cashflow.

As most of the markets for legal services are contracting and earnings therefore reducing, it is hardly a surprise to see significant redundancy programmes in law firms and even less of a surprise to see that recruitment has been drastically reduced in this recession.

Before the recession really started to have a significantly negative impact, and over perhaps as many as the last ten years, one could take literally any week in the year and the three editions of the UK's biggest circulation weekly legal journals (The Law Society Gazette, The Lawyer and Legal Week) would each have carried 15 to 20 full pages of job advertisements.

The roles advertised would be for lawyers in all sectors of the profession, in-house, in law firms, for all seniorities, in the UK and overseas. This amounts to probably around 250 new job advertisements each and every week; but now those same journals are so thin they might be carrying less than 25% of the roles they used to advertise.

This is an astonishing change, which, if it carries on, will have significant structural implications for universities and law schools as well. Students will no doubt think twice about incurring significant debt when competition for places in law firms will be even more intense than it is now.

This contraction in the recruitment market, apart from having a potentially seriously damaging impact on our teaching institutions and (more frivolously) on print journalism for the legal sector, is indicative of three highly significant points:

1. First, the legal services market in its traditional shape is clearly contracting; for businesses that use lawyers there are fewer deals to be done and fewer products to launch.

2. Second, businesses have less money to spend on external counsel and the budgets that in-house legal teams might once have had to spend on legal fees have contracted markedly. As a result prices are falling and law firms that might once have been described as less fashionable are winning business they would not expect to have won before.

3. Third, and linked to the second point, in-house teams are bringing more work in-house. In part this is self-preservation and is linked to a desire to show that they are a valuable and value-adding asset to their businesses doing meaningful work; in part it is saving the money that would otherwise have been paid to the law firms.

There is quite clearly significantly less traditional legal work in the market and what work there is being rebalanced among the different external providers of the service (who are competing mostly on price) and law firms and in-house teams. So not only is there less work, but there is a very strong push to reduce the cost of the activity that is undertaken; this in turn inevitably has a significant impact on the cost-base of law firms. As a result many law firms have had to embark on one or more rounds of redundancy consultation, cutting back on apparently unproductive teams and laying off lawyers where the work does not presently justify the headcount.

In some respects of course this is very much usual business practice and up to a point should be business as usual even in the best of times. The question that would be in the minds of many non-lawyer businesses would be "Why should law firms be immune from the constant internal debate about managing costs within income?"

Indeed I used to work for a chief executive who told me he would look to reduce some headcount in boom times because it kept everyone on their toes and he hated complacency; but in more difficult times he would hire some people, because he wanted the competition to believe he could expand his business at their expense. So while redundancies in the legal profession have been as rare as hens' teeth since the early 1990s, redundancies per se are not necessarily indicative of anything more than the sensible realignment of supply and demand.

On a broader front, however, considering the market as a whole and the countless stories of redundancies and lay-offs, the perception of many clients of the profession is that losing junior lawyers and support staff and the deferment of trainees is an indication not of strategic planning or thoughtful realignment, but of preserving partner drawings at previous record levels.

For many years now it has baffled a significant number of clients that the press and public relations teams in so many law firms have wanted to loudly proclaim the often extraordinarily high PPP (profit per partner) figure earned by their key employees. It was as if the law firms believed that their clients would interpret these always significant year-on-year improvements in the financial well-being of partners as a sure sign of fabulous improvements in service. In fact most clients saw the ritual chest thumping of the law firms as a sure-fire indication that their fees would be on the rise again!

It is just possible, however, that we are now turning a corner. To begin with there appears to be a dawning realisation that annual seven figure drawings are not going to be a realistic aspiration for future generations of equity partners. This will instead be viewed as a distant memory of an age when excess had a heavy price to pay. Secondly some firms, thank goodness, are now engaging with all their staff and evaluating the worth of all their human resources recognising that this plays very strongly with clients.

This last point makes perfect sense. It has been a significant point of client relationship management theory to ensure that there are multiple points of contact between law firm and client. The traditional "bow-tie" of relationship partner and client contact meeting at a single point of engagement was rightly discouraged for its selfish vulnerabilities.

A firm that has encouraged and developed multiple contacts with clients means multiple relationships, even friendships, all of which can potentially create and embed value for the law firms.

If these relationships, however, are dismantled in an economic recession with what are perceived to be harsh decisions or harsh processes, then the law firm risks its disaffected lawyers and staff telling their client friends and contacts and as a result risks seeing value haemorrhage. Before too long the strategic decision to make someone redundant – badly handled or for the wrong reasons – is a reputational risk issue for the law firm with untold ramifications.

I would also like to share one small observation to provide a genuinely positive example and it concerns my experience of visiting the Birmingham office of one of the national law firms. On arrival in their modest but functional city centre reception area, one is met by two security personnel; but this is not the surly, uncommunicative type of security presence – these guys are unfailingly polite and cheerful. They smile, look pleased to see you, welcome you by name and always ensure an efficient and cheerful entrance to the firm's main reception area…and when you leave the office later, they remember your name and wish you good day.

It makes for an understated, but warm, greeting that says a great deal about the tone of voice of the firm as a whole. As most clients cannot form judgements on the quality of the legal expertise they are offered, such small points as the way visitors are received can count out of all proportion to their real value, contributing to the reasons why clients value the experience and ensuring they will return comfortably time and time again.

The "meet and greet" by the security team in question is as impressive as any welcome to any firm I know and I would be deeply disappointed if ever the firm decided to make cost saving changes to this particular aspect of its general office overhead.

It is also, may I suggest, increasingly significant for many clients to know that their firms are investing in people who are part of the relationship experience, rather than (perhaps) in overblown and rather bewildering art installations. As one General Counsel said to me,

"I am frankly embarrassed to take my boss to see the firm; their "aircraft hangar" sized reception area would be enough storage space for us to have half a warehouse on a light industrial estate – but this is in central London, at goodness knows what floor cost and it is used by them for four sofas, two trees and a fountain – and the firm have the nerve to talk to me about wanting to provide value for money... it is, and they are, completely ridiculous."

The approach of the firm with the welcoming security team is perhaps a more sure-footed statement of self-confidence in these more straitened times.

26. Client Relationship Development

Ihave always wanted to write about business development for law firms, but written from a client-centric perspective. This article sets out a comprehensive and detailed concept for developing business opportunities based on practical and not theoretical steps that any law firm could take. It is not rocket science; it never was. For the majority of law firms, for the foreseeable future, the key to current and future success will be the systematic, thoughtful and planned development of relationships to deliver sustainable and profitable business opportunities.

But while it sounds easy, "old hat" even, it isn't easy and it needs a very significant effort indeed, unlike anything we have done before. In the past there has been some investment from the profession in this area; there is plenty of training, plenty of expensive IT, but I am certain there is not enough strategic insight to make it hang together and actually deliver. To begin with let's not talk again of CRM (Client Relationship Management); it sounds passive and suffocating. Instead we should talk about CRD (Client Relationship Development); which is much more about seeking progression and opportunity, and is driven by proactive thoughtful engagement.

CRD is not a by-numbers-approach or one-size-fits-all. Nor is it a panacea...because nothing will succeed without the thoughtfulness, hard work and discipline of the lawyers still to use their judgement. Nor is it guaranteed to succeed; think of it as a healthy diet – not a fad for a few weeks, but a lifestyle choice for the long term.

Done well, CRD can become an essential business discipline and possibly the only predictable means by which any firm will measurably improve the likelihood of winning new business and, most importantly, the profitability of existing business. CRD should really be

131

focused on keeping and growing the existing portfolio of work. The hidden cost to firms of clients moving away is rarely quantified, but is an increasing strain in such a competitive environment.

To be successful CRD requires great implementation, lifting what otherwise is just another three letter acronym into something that can actually make a difference to business. There are four cornerstones to implementation:

1. The IT processes that will support your CRD systems must be robust and well tested – so IT is essential, but CRD should not be seen as just an IT system.

2. The internal training programme you develop to support your CRD systems and processes must be well attended, collaborative, participative, interesting and useful – but CRD is not just a training course.

3. The management information that is collected about your CRD systems and processes must be accurate, accessible and timely – but CRD is not just a statistical tool.

4. The marketing and business development support in your firm must be aligned with this initiative and enthusiastically supported by the lawyers so that you are able to count every opportunity that your CRD systems and processes reveal – but CRD is not just marketing.

Client Relationship Development has to be in the law firm's "DNA", part of every activity, interwoven into the fabric of the business, not just enabled but also embedded. Leaders of any law firm today should want everyone in their business from the most senior to the most junior - every business support team, every lawyer, every management board member, every secretary, every administrator, every librarian, and every trainee - to be thinking about how they contribute to making the firm work more effectively for their colleagues and for and on behalf of the firm's clients.

CRD implementation therefore requires the firm to have the "tools" to deliver and set out below I have written about six toolkits; they are linked together, but they do not have to be seen as sequential. They could, in fact, be considered like the six sides of a cube; each side supports the strength of the shape, no one side is more important than another, but each side has its own unique albeit dependent place in the structure. The analogy helps to define a genuinely multi-dimensional approach – one not just defined by processes or systems, but one which depends on thoughtfulness, innovation and creativity as well.

At the heart of the concept is the need to see that clients are not institutions, or brands or fancy addresses; clients are people, real people who make real judgements about the quality of service they receive, especially when they are under pressure, especially therefore like now.

What is needed then is a mix of clear strategy, energy, insight and leadership that has the potential to bring about a self-enforcing, adaptable model for business retention, business growth and relationship development, but a model as well that adapts to client needs and which seeks their engagement in every aspect of the law firm proposition.

The six toolkits described below illustrate points of engagement and activity; there is genuine flexibility in how to use the tools and how much complexity or sophistication each needs to become effective in your world. I do not necessarily recommend each individual approach, but I do recommend that each toolkit, in some form or another, should have a place in your Client Relationship Development strategy.

The six toolkits are:

1. Internal review for client evaluation

2. A communications strategy

3. Preparing for the new business pitch

4. Understanding client needs

5. Undertaking client facing reviews

6. Developing behaviours and values for success

1. Internal review for client evaluation

The objective is to create the guidance necessary for teams to establish the potential new value in an existing relationship and the corrective actions needed to retain a client and then to generate the business development plan for the client. The internal review tool should be developed to comprise a comprehensive template of actions and cross-references to internal/external resources. Such a tool will assist in understanding the current profitability of a client, their strategic and reference value as well as the potential for growth.

Sample items in this toolkit might be:

1. Definitions for internal roles. The role of relationship manager should be defined to include key deliverables and described in terms of tasks to be performed as well as in aspirational terms – and there should also be a framework for identifying colleagues who need to be involved in the review meetings.

2. Develop a concept of "contact alert" where, if one person hears something about a client/sector, this is then emailed to all in the team, leading to an assessment of impact/ threats/opportunities.

3. A key question is "Whom do we know?" This should be updated regularly with a maintained list of the deputies to all senior positions and the names of PAs of all senior roles. Also, any gaps should be identified and assessed.

4. Plan low level interaction. How often should key contacts receive a message? Did you know that every day every human being in the UK receives 8000 marketing messages? Think about it, 8000 times we are touched by an advert, a brand, a headline, a value, an experience. In-house legal teams are so used to the intensity of marketing that they have become very sophisticated buyers. Legal service providers are still some way off the pace of product placement, viral

marketing, PR etc…frankly anything that you can do more of will be an improvement.

2. Communications

The objective is to create guidance and templates for internal and external communications. Sample items in this toolkit are:

1. How to devise a communication protocol with the client. A communication template should be provided with supporting details: the expected communication channels and protocols, the contact points, how new contact points are introduced, the preferred medium for communication, when and how this changes, the escalation process, how instructions are to be received and verified, when social contact is acceptable, the sort of hospitality that is appropriate, the conflicts policy - and so on.

2. Emphasis on personal contact. Telephone and face-to-face contact needs to be encouraged. Personal interest information of the contact needs to be captured (football team supported, number of children) - not for corny/forced conversation, but just to help the team see the client as three-dimensional and not a brand name.

3. Definition of roles. Key to the protocol is who does what and when. From the client side, know who makes the decisions, who are the key stakeholders and who can only refer work.

4. Internal communication planning. We also need to know how we meet people from different teams. Referring work happens when we have good internal networks and we know and trust our colleagues. Internal networking is essential and should be developed and expected of everyone.

5. Client Information management. What is gathered and what is done with it? This is partly an issue of definition of roles, but also lends itself to reiterating

the process discipline point. We have to make this process "live" and not just let it become a well-intentioned but largely ignored set of hopes and notes. The regular contact and the checking that contact is effective must become second nature. Reminder and prompt messages may help, but there is also a valuable role to be played by the IT support teams.

3. New business pitch

The objective of this tool is to demonstrate how to prepare for and deliver an outstanding pitch; the components are guidance on team selection, role planning, research and, crucially, rehearsal.

The rise of the procurement function in both the public and private sectors (or at the very least the introduction of more procurement disciplines) means that this initiative has to have real investment. In this regard, then, consider developing scenario planning tools, a detailed analysis of a previous real pitch turned into a case study for others to learn from, and practical realistic training.

It is a perennial criticism of this sort of approach that the materials exist in a vacuum, unconnected with the day-to-day realities of a busy office. In each situation therefore ensure you link these ideas to existing internal materials and personnel with the expertise to help. In other words make them work, make them relevant, make them accessible and useful.

Areas that you should ensure are covered in this process should include the following ten points. It is clearly a significant undertaking:

1. Instruction initiation – in other words, understanding where and how business comes into the firm (what is the relative success of, for example, repeat work from existing clients, direct and indirect marketing, client referral, directories, outside consultants etc.?). As a result, can the law firm identify ways to increase the probability of work being delivered through these

channels and to invest more in the most successful routes to market?

2. The kick-off meeting to decide whether we "really, really, really want to do this" should have a formulaic feel to it to help avoid speculative "punts" and develop more consistency. At the very least ensure that there is a common agenda, that key stakeholders present and that you understand the direct and indirect operational and strategic consequences of proceeding with or declining the opportunity.

3. Ensure a consistent and detailed analysis of the client's Request for Information/Purchase questionnaire. Be prepared to engage with it fully and in detail or risk looking as though you have photocopied chucks off your website and that you really couldn't care less for the opportunity.

4. Always prepare an internal briefing paper describing the strengths, weaknesses, threats and opportunities presented by the prospective pitch. Ensure this is widely circulated to elicit buy-in (or otherwise) from colleagues. Particularly for the larger client, the more there is an enthusiastic firm-wide approach to the process, the better the chance of success.

5. At this point internal roles can be more clearly defined and the necessary internal and external communication strategy can be defined so that the law firm appears joined-up, consistent and aligned.

6. Then the research, fact-finding and positioning can be developed and agreed and this in turn helps to ensure that the firm can present a more innovative, thoughtful and directed pitch response. Further, and still at this early stage, it should be possible to decide what the key decision points will be (scope of work, its cost, the resources to be deployed and the value-add to be offered etc.) and then to define any consequential steps you may have to take throughout the process.

7. Additionally ask the question, "What are the other internal issues?" Are there, for example, other bids within the firm to co-ordinate (existing or predicted)? In addition what are the implications for existing clients and contacts? – consider not just the question of formal conflicts, but also consider perceptions that may have to be managed in the market/sector.

8. The client's interests and concerns should also be mapped, discussed and agreed internally to make the pitch process as empathetic and bespoke as possible. Can you, for example, engage directly/indirectly with the client to ask questions, explore options, eliminate anything unnecessary etc.?

9. The pitch document is then delivered. Ensure it is delivered in time, to all the people who should receive it and in the desired format. I would also suggest that at this point it is a good time to thank everyone involved in the firm.

10. Win, lose or draw, there should be post-pitch analysis with lessons learned and actions developed for immediate follow up. As part of this consider whether any more communication is needed with colleagues and always make time to discuss outcomes with the learning and development teams in the firm.

Scoping the process in this way can make it look over-engineered - that must be left to your judgment - but the main point to make is that there must be a process so that the firm will apply a consistent and more disciplined approach to the business of pitch preparation and (hopefully) make better decisions to reject some opportunities while improving prospects for success in the activity it does pursue.

4. Needs analysis

In this section the objective is to create and then maintain a step-by-step guide to increasing the competency and capability of teams to operate the Client Relationship

Development strategy. This is in effect an entirely internal facing toolkit.

Ensure there is a means to ascertain both personal and team-wide training needs analysis. Focus especially on soft skills, including networking skills, presentation skills, relationship management and influencing skills. This is not client specific, but is about ensuring that all lawyers get access to training and coaching to help equip them for the roles they must perform. Consider this a collaborative exercise, designed to make a real difference to performance and not something that is about "ticking boxes".

The five areas to be covered include:

1. Research thoroughly where to source your internal and external training support. Maintain a file of articles and press clippings, prompt activity with regular diary reminders, include online links on your desk-top to consultants, establish authority levels for supplier engagement and take references for consultants and suppliers not previously engaged before. In effect create and update your own trainer directory.

2. Create coaching and mentoring opportunities. What might this look like in the firm and how would it work? This doesn't have to be too formalised, but it is a fundamental part of anyone's development to feel that someone they regard well is taking a personal and helpful interest in their career. I am probably too much of an evangelist in this area, but having had a mentor for more than twenty years it is my passionate view that mentoring should be institutionalised and made compulsory.

3. Take the time to thoroughly understand your own internal systems – What do the processes do now? What is their potential for development and improvement? What are the barriers to systems improvement? How can you encourage a culture of continuous improvement? This point is about

ensuring there is a strategy that can work so that your plans do not just exist on paper.

4. Ensure all your internal resources are aligned to your strategy. Share information, invite comment, make plain your objectives, celebrate your successes and ensure that when things go less well that the reasons for this are understood fully – not to blame anyone or anything, but simply to illuminate how to improve process and engagement going forward. The more open you are to feedback, the easier it is to make change, because change prompted by feedback automatically carries much more support.

5. Client facing review

The fifth objective is to create the template and identify the resources needed for an effective review meeting with an existing client. Obtaining feedback from clients is more than an exercise in good PR; this is essential intelligence for your business development; it protects you from surprises and gives you opportunity for growth. Done well, it will provide rich insight and will help shape your future strategy.

There are five areas to be covered in this toolkit:

1. How to set up meetings with clients. Establishing whom to approach and how to persuade them that a meeting is worth their while. Develop consistent, accessible and simple support materials that should include, for example, draft agendas and sample email/letters/telephone scripts. The more this is made routine, the easier it is to establish the programme

2. Devising the objectives ahead of the meeting. This should include identifying the key positives and negatives and ensuring you can understand what is driving both. What would the firm then suggest that might improve the quality of the experience for the client? Are there areas where the firm can save money for the client? Can the firm demonstrate that

it is taking time to understand the commercial issues facing the client? How can the firm show that it cares without that being seen as clichéd?

3. Consider also obtaining structured feedback from your own teams so that you can gauge how the lawyers and the support personnel feel the service is delivered and how they are instructed. Feedback here can make a direct impact on process improvement. This then gives you the means to identify the gaps between the lawyer's perception and the client feedback. A resulting "gap" analysis will also result in identifying priorities to be addressed.

4. Importantly make sure time is given to interpret feedback and to obtain commitment to take action in those areas where improvement is needed. Often clients perceive that, while a good deal of structure is evident to collect feedback, there is very little structure to inform them how their feedback is interpreted and what actions have followed. This is a powerful opportunity to show commitment to the client and to build value in the relationship and it must not be lost - it is such a straightforward winning opportunity for the law firm.

5. Finally, make sure there is always opportunity to report to colleagues within the firm on the current client status and how the relationship might be developed going forward. The more this information is shared, the easier it is to gain commitment to collective activity.

6. Behaviours and values

This final toolkit is a little more intangible, focusing as it does on behaviours and values. It does, however, represent a vital frame-working analysis.

For example what are the types of people that do well in your firm? What do they stand for? How do they operate? What behaviours does the firm encourage? What behaviours does the firm discourage? What is the ideal client experience of working with the firm?

The areas to be covered will include the following five activities:

1. Induction training. Even in the first few weeks of a new start, there should be clear and consistent information available on what is expected in terms of behaviours and values. This should be reinforced not just for lawyers but for all the support teams as well.

2. Best practice case studies. How can a trainee in your firm make a difference? What is expected of personnel in the post-room, on reception etc.? What should people be doing at different stages of their careers? It probably sounds contrived when it is condensed into a short paragraph, but making people better is not a contrivance and the more the firm can do to help people improve, the more improvement the firm will see.

3. Ethical policies and codes of conduct. What is the aspirational and exemplary behaviour you seek? Conversely, what is always unacceptable? Include in this conflict training. How are conflicts managed? What steps must be taken and how? How does the firm inform clients? This is often a tricky area, but well managed it will speak volumes for the firm.

4. Appraisal and assessment criteria. For some time to come I suspect that targets for billable time are still going to be a key indicator to a successful career for the lawyers; but if business development is to be truly valued, then credit must be given for good business development activity. I would also recommend linking at least some activity to CSR and other long term goals that help build the reputation of the firm.

5. The firm should have competency frameworks for all the different levels and grades within the firm from trainee to associate to senior associate to partner, and for the non -lawyer roles as well. This is not about

creating HR nirvana, but about developing accessible and practical guidance on how to make progress in the firm. Roles should be defined not by tasks and reporting lines but by behaviours and competencies. Coaching and mentoring programmes should be part and parcel of the firm's approach to embedding the values it believes in.

Developing the concept and the content

Client Relationship Development is a much more dynamic and hopeful way to encourage engagement with clients and contacts than some more traditional ideas of client relationship management.

If these activities are pursued, then they can help any firm maintain and build business opportunity, but now it is the firm's next steps that are the most important. The Client Relationship Development concept is potentially interesting, certainly workable; it is, however, unfinished to the extent that the detail that populates each side of the cube must be developed and made credible by you.

27. Ever wondered why?

Ever wondered why stuff happens? Ever wondered why, when you were just reaching the point in your career when things could be getting easier, when all your hard work was about to pay off, then, suddenly, the legal services market came to a shuddering halt and all the old certainties seemed more like empty promises?

I think it is doubtful that things will ever be as they used to be; but are you thinking now that the pear-shaped nature of your lot is a rum deal, or are you thinking that when the world gets a bit shaken up, there are perhaps going to be new opportunities and new reputations to be made? It can be a mistake to wonder why; sometimes the best thing to do is to think instead about the "what next?" and the challenges and opportunities to come. In this article I want to explore straightforward and easy to take steps that will help us make the best of whatever cards we have been dealt.

Five steps for self-preservation

On the assumption that for now you are sticking with being a lawyer (!), these five steps build out a proposition that is about values as well as expertise:

1. Exemplary service counts because you are very expensive and service should be exemplary. What else in life would you pay for that costs thousands of pounds and comes with no guarantee of anything - not outcome, cost or timeline? The least you can do is be brilliant at managing expectation and being thoughtful about the client.

2. Be collaborative internally and externally; sometimes you have to share with others before others will share with you. Be generous with your time and take an interest in what is going on around you. Where

can you help? How you make others look good? What is great about your business? What could be improved?

3. Give away more time than you should; a bit dangerous to say this so boldly, but sometimes not charging for something (especially when the gesture has been volunteered) can speak more of your commitment, understanding and sense of priority than all the fine words you could ever read in a marketing brochure.

4. Shape a role where your integrity is at the heart of things. Being bigger than your work is not about arrogance or selfishness; on the contrary it is a selfless regard for your client, your practice and your colleagues, always doing the right thing and behaving in the right way – despite the obvious provocations and temptations.

5. Set targets that are more than just about how long you spend on things. Bully for you if you clock up 1400 chargeable hours, but how are you a better lawyer, better colleague, better communicator, better negotiator for all that experience …and how would your client know?

Five steps to avoid self-destruction

Legal advice is not an exact science. It is like a multi-dimensional dance where the music, the venue, the steps and the people all have significant characteristics and where those characteristics can change radically or imperceptibly.

The biggest mistake you will ever make is to think that, if you get the law right (whatever that means), everything else will be plain sailing. Five elephant traps to avoid:

1. However clever your clients seem, they will not understand or care how hard you work to provide the solutions they need. Consider how many people and processes it takes to design, build and test a new car; consider the zillions of pounds needed to build, equip and staff an assembly plant; consider the vast

network of sales teams, showrooms and transporters needed to keep stocks of vehicles close to the people who might want to buy them; how much of that do you think about when you nip down the road to the shops? Your clients feel the same way about you. So don't assume your clients think about the value of what you do until they get the bill.

2. Winning new businesses is not always about past performance. It counts quite a lot obviously, but winning new business has much to do with two other factors:

    a. What the clients think about the immediate future (Is it different from the immediate past?)

    b. Who they believe will deliver value for them in their new future?

It is so easy to lose out by making ill-founded assumptions based on the fact that you have worked diligently and well on many matters, if you are not tuned into how your client feels today about tomorrow.

3. Linked to this last point is the very tedious fact that it is easier to promise the earth when you are the new kid on the block! Your competitors will promise to be cheaper, more efficient, cleverer and more beautiful than you, because they can make assumptions and the client can dream; but you have a track record of lumpy reality. Therefore, keep your relationships vital and fresh, assume nothing and do not find yourself usurped by interloping fancy-pants newcomers.

4. Never, ever let your clients think you have other more important work to do for someone else. They will know that you have more important work from time to time, but a parent should never have a favourite child, and you must never let your clients think there is a hierarchy of preference - otherwise you risk one of two responses:

a. They will take comfort from someone else where they fell more loved.

b. Even if they want to give you work, they will think twice about doing so out of a concern for your well-being.

Either way, it is a daft place to put yourself...so don't do it.

5. Your clients expect you to know everything and they therefore judge you harshly when you slip up - misspell the chief executive's name, for example, and this can be extrapolated into "Well if they don't know that, what else don't they know?" Before you realise, the client has you consigned to a place labelled "useless"! Small points count because clients want you to be cleverer than they are; they want you to be brilliant. When clients realise that they know more than you do, the mystique is gone, your cover blown and suddenly the clients feel they should question everything.

I am now of an age when the language of my children excludes my understanding, but invites my concern. In everything I do, therefore, I must try to avoid sounding too grumpy or appearing to have all the answers. That said I would however like to suggest five actions for all lawyers to take that I believe will help to build momentum in their business development planning:

Five steps for momentum

1. Always have a plan to do something to develop an existing relationship or a new contact. Who are your top ten clients? What makes them so good and you so good for them? Can you analyse what works well and replicate it elsewhere? What will you do with each of your top ten clients this month that will confirm the quality and standing of the relationship?

2. Put yourself in the line of fire. Volunteer to run a seminar, to create a networking event, to do some client feedback work, to peer-review a colleague's work. Do this not because you are a goody two-shoes,

147

but because you need profile and experience to be successful. It is rare for those who sit in the shadows to gain profile or experience.

3. Know your weaknesses and expose them. I'm not big on self help books, but one that I turn to occasionally is "Feel the Fear and do it Anyway" by Susan Jeffers. Compensating for our weaknesses makes us lopsided, improving our weaknesses gives us more balance, The more you do to address your weaknesses and to discuss them openly with those you trust, the quicker and more progressive will be your improvement.

4. Help a colleague in need. It is such a selfish world that to take time out of your schedule to support a colleague is immensely powerful and will underline the strength of the team. There will be days when you need help too; so invest in the bank of goodwill and feel more comfortable when you have to make a withdrawal.

5. Build your pro bono practice. The landscape for legal services is changing so rapidly that it is easy to overlook things that ought to be obvious. In a new world not so far away those businesses that can offer legal services will be many and varied; what will make your practice stand out will be linked to your brand and the values attributed to that brand. Pro bono work speaks to integrity, community, respect and thoughtfulness – hard to imagine a more powerful set of values.

Five big steps

Finally, let's now take a big picture view; five issues the profession should address (and which you should therefore address as well) to be credible in the new world order that will develop from the global recession and the advent of new structures permitted by the Legal Services Act:

1. Whatever the structure or the brand of the business you work in, clients will want to be able to trust your judgement. If the profession is to have a future it needs to exemplify what trusting judgement means. Whatever you do, never undermine the fact that people value trust more than almost anything you can think of.

2. Technology will accelerate the pace of change and will provide solutions that diminish the value of one-to-one interaction; this will permit lower-cost options, quick answers, more self-help and much more interaction. You need to be an architect in this world, not a grumpy bystander.

3. Your ability to be considered by your colleagues and clients as a rounded commercial adviser, confident with numbers and with a head for strategy, will open doors that are usually closed. Your personal development programme must open this possibility for you; if not, you risk being left behind…a floppy disc to others' digital download.

4. Retaining and developing strong relationships will give you a platform to evolve and grow; this must be your first strategic priority. Businesses must not chase new markets like chasing butterflies, but develop and then believe in a proposition that defines their excellence and which creates certainty for clients and colleagues alike.

5. Challenge old notions, but do so within a framework of integrity - hourly billing, conflicts management, traditional career paths, risk and reward. The profession has little choice other than to reinvent itself in the next five years.

Ever wondered why you were given such a great opportunity to do something really very special?

The best you can be is a work in progress, not a destination. The best service you can provide is a constantly shifting complex set of issues and emotions;

your emotional intelligence has to be finely honed and part of what makes you the person you are. Invest in yourself.

And a final thought to end on: if you can deliver in this environment, you will be able to deliver in any environment.

Acknowledgements

I am once again indebted to Geoffrey Williams, Chairman of LBC Wise Counsel, mentor, editor and, above all, friend, for his patience and care in editing these articles.

About the author

Paul Gilbert is the Chief Executive and founder of LBC Wise Counsel, a specialist management consultancy for law firms and in-house legal teams with a particular focus on change management, relationship management, strategic planning and personal development.

LBC Wise Counsel predominantly acts for in-house teams in the UK and Europe with some activity in North America too. In addition Paul regularly works with law firms at partner conferences, at training events and in a consulting capacity on topics such as business development and relationship management.

LBC Wise Counsel is the company behind the ground-breaking LBCambridgeTM spring and summer schools for in-house lawyers at Queens' College, Cambridge.

(www.lbcwisecounsel.com/cambridge)

For six years Paul was a Council Member of the England & Wales Law Society and was elected to the Society's Main Management Board. He now writes and lectures widely on the changing face of the legal profession, including the threats and the opportunities following the passing of legislation in the UK that will facilitate significant change in the way legal services are organised and delivered.

Previously Paul was General Counsel in two major UK financial services companies and he has also held positions as chairman and chief executive of the national in-house lawyers Commerce & Industry Group.

He is currently a Trustee of LawWorks, the UK's national pro bono charity.

The End

Lightning Source UK Ltd.
Milton Keynes UK
UKOW05f0620221116
288207UK00001B/39/P